plugged in

Becoming a Screen-Savvy Family

How to Navigate a Media-Saturated World—
and Why We Should

Paul Asay, General Editor

FOCUS
ON THE FAMILY.

*A Focus on the Family resource
published by Tyndale House Publishers*

T0035921

Contents

The Power of Story

Paul Asay

"SO, DO YOU REALLY COUNT SWEAR WORDS?"
In my work at Focus on the Family's *Plugged In*, I get that question a lot—especially from other movie reviewers.

My secular cohorts don't worry about tabulating profanities. They don't worry about excessive bathroom humor or tawdry double entendres or just how many beheadings a medieval battle scene might include. They don't take pages upon pages of notes at movie screenings, detailing everything from worldview issues to wardrobe choices. So it's natural they'd think me a little . . . odd, sitting way up in the back row of a theater with a light-up pen, taking notes about language and violence and sexuality.

1

Those other reviewers, who work for secular newspapers or websites or blogs or podcasts, are there for one primary reason: to tell their readers/listeners/users whether a given movie is any good. Sure, some write for specific audiences: horror aficionados, maybe; or sci-fi fans; or political conservatives; or those from the LGBT community. But the core questions these reviewers try to answer are, ultimately, pretty simple: *Did I like the movie? Will you?* They're fundamentally subjective questions.

Plugged In's reviewers try to answer those questions, sure. We all appreciate a well-crafted movie. We like good acting and fantastic cinematography and eye-popping special effects as much as anyone. But we don't stop with aesthetic quality—that's more or less just a starting point. After all, we have other questions to answer: *Is this movie a good fit for you? Is it right for your family? Do its messages line up with the Bible? What is it trying to teach us?*

Yes, like other reviewers, we're trying to help you tell whether a movie is "good." But for us, that word is multi-layered. It's not enough for a movie to be *good* like a bacon cheeseburger. We want to know whether it's good *for* you, like a kale salad. (And if it's kale that *tastes* like a bacon cheeseburger? All the better.) It goes beyond whether a movie works: We talk about how the movie might be working *on* you.

Our jobs go well beyond movies, of course, even though many of you reading this book are aware of *Plugged In* mainly through our movie reviews. We critique pretty much every form of media entertainment there is—from television to books to video games to YouTube channels. We dig into social media and technology as well.

But if there's one overarching thing we cover—one word that gathers everything we do under one colorful umbrella—it's *story*. Stories told in print and song and especially on screen; the stories we share online; the stories we continually find new, creative ways to tell, and how those creative ways might change the stories themselves.

So instead of being asked *Why do you count swear words?*, we might well be asked *Why do you care so much about these stories?* Because, really, that encompasses the swear-word question and the dozens of other questions we hear. It explains why fourteen-year-old kids (whose parents make entertainment choices based on our reviews) sometimes curse the mere mention of our name. It explains why sometimes we have to spoil certain plot points in our reviews (even though we try not to do so unnecessarily). It explains why we do this strange, strange work—and why we think that watching movies and telling you about them is actually kind of important.

And for me, the answer truly begins—as many stories do—in the beginning.

STUFF AND STORY

Most scientists will tell you that we are made of *stuff*: skin and bones, water and carbon, protons and electrons. A chemist would say that it's all pretty much the *same* stuff: Ninety-nine percent of the human body is made of oxygen, carbon, hydrogen, nitrogen, calcium, and phosphorus. A biologist would observe that those elements are the building blocks for everything from our skin to our brains, from our livers to our lymph nodes. And we don't typically get a lot of variation there. One heart may be slightly larger than another, but it's not like any of us get, say, six of them.

Geneticists identify a few more differences: our sex, the color of our skin, the shape of our noses. Humans can look very different from one another, yet the geneticist is quick to remind us that 99.9 percent of your genes—no matter who you are—are identical to mine. From the standpoint of science, if we were LEGO pieces, we'd *all* be boring ol' two-by-four bricks—only each of us would be an ever-so-slightly different shade of green or blue.

Yet the variation we see in each other can take our collective breath away. We are so different in how we think and act, how we grieve and celebrate, how we pray and vote. Sometimes even folks from our very own gene pool can feel as though they come from a completely different planet. At Thanksgiving, we may discover very good reasons to avoid making fun of *Ancient Aliens* when Aunt Esther's within earshot.

Yes, we're made of mostly the same stuff. But dig a little deeper—underneath that stuff—and you'll find a deeper, more important truth: We're made of stories. And those stories make us who we are.

We are who we are because of what we've experienced. What happened to us at the age of four impacts how we think at age forty. These events shape how we think, how we act, how we relate to others. And they obviously impact how others relate to us.

I think it's both beautiful and illustrative that the universe itself is a story, told by the ultimate Storyteller. "Let there be light," God said, as the first book of the Bible tells us (Genesis 1:3). And it was so. *Let there be land and sea, let there be birds and beasts, let there be you and me.* And it was so. He *spoke* everything we know—perhaps everything we *can* know—into reality. Our cosmos began, essentially, with *once upon a time*—a time before anyone could count it, a time without sun or moon or stars. It was the first *once*, the first *story*. And from that first came all the stories that followed.

When God molded us from dust, He not only breathed His life into us but also blessed us with a love of story. Because it's through stories (among other things) that God shows His love for us. It's through stories that we learned to love Him. He made us, I think, uniquely attuned to learn through stories—to be influenced by them.

The Bible is, essentially, a book of stories—crisply told, full of heroes and villains, littered with both the familiar and the exotic. Some are as simple as children's fables. Others can be as multilayered and enigmatic as Russian novels. Some stories are both—with our experience of them changing (as it will with any truly great story) in depth and complexity as our understanding increases.

Even Jesus taught through stories, using everything from mustard seeds to prodigal sons in His parables. And we are storytellers too. Our stories separate us from the animals that share our space. Birds might sing. Chimpanzees use tools. Whales have some language abilities. But storytelling? As far as we know, it is unique to us—our ability to share our stories with each other, to bond over them and even make up our own.

The Bible tells us that we're made in God's image. But perhaps the word *image* refers to something beyond mere physical likeness. I wonder whether the word reflects the reality that we, too, engage in small acts and echoes of Creation. While only God can speak the universe into being, we *can* tell stories. We can imagine worlds filled with dragons or fairies. We can weave tales filled with hard-boiled detectives or corrupt kings or brave starship captains. We can, in our own way, create something that wasn't there before.

When we tell stories, we follow the example of the Creator of everything, whether we acknowledge it or not. We don't create mountains and bushes and field mice from nothing, as God did. But we still follow humbly in His glorious footsteps.

Madeleine L'Engle, author of *A Wrinkle in Time*, wrote, "All of us who have given birth to a baby, to a story, know that it is ultimately mystery, closely knit to God's own creative activities which did not stop at the beginning of the universe. God is constantly creating, in us, through us, with us, and to co-create with God is our human calling."[1]

But here's the thing: When God created the universe, before sin had a chance to do its work, He could see that it was *good*. Creation reflected Him, and Him alone. It embodied His boundless creativity, His measureless love.

But with us? It's a different story. Literally.

FALLEN FAIRY TALES

As we know, it didn't take long for sin to take Creation and twist it. We lost Eden when we lost our way. Our own stories—in other words, our lives—are filled with strife and pain and so much failure. We may begin our stories with "Once upon a time," but rarely do we find that our endings are, without blemish, "happily ever after." Even the best of us can't manage that outcome.

When I was a kid, I loved reading about David. What Christian kid wouldn't? David was one of the few biblical youngsters who did much of anything, it seemed to me back then. And, man, did he do something pretty cool and wildly violent (always a perk in Bible stories for me as a kid). In 1 Samuel 17, we read about his most famous exploit.

A Philistine named Goliath—a literal giant—was trash-talking the entire Israelite army. And even though King Saul promised a mountain of treasure and his daughter's hand in marriage to anyone who'd kill the guy, not one of his men dared face Goliath in single combat. (Who could blame them?) David volunteered to take on this, ahem, *giant* task. But the Israelite armor was too heavy for him, and the sword's sheath dragged along the ground when he put it on (or so I extrapolated from the text when I was a kid). So he tossed it all aside and instead fought Goliath with a sling and five smooth stones.

He just needed one of those stones to take down the towering Philistine.

David was brave and courageous—a real hero in that story. And even at my young age, I got the point: If you place your faith in God, nothing—not even giants—can stand in your way. Nice and tidy, that. It was a happily-ever-after sort of story.

Or so it was if you didn't continue reading.

David's story is inherently tied to King Saul's, and all the political and palace intrigue that followed. It's tied to the story of Bathsheba, the woman David lusted after, and Uriah, her husband, whom David sent to his death. It's tied to that of David's rebellious son, Absalom, who was done in by his much-admired hair (2 Samuel 18:9). King David's last words to his successor, Solomon, were to kill an old enemy of his. "Bring his gray head down to the grave in blood" (1 Kings 2:9). And with that, the Bible says, David rested with his ancestors.

David was a man after God's own heart, as the Bible often reminds us. And yet he was a sinner surrounded by sinners, prone to tears and anger and something close to despair. David's story reminds us, in the end, that we are all fallen creatures in a fallen world. Whatever happiness we taste is salted with tears—often tears of our own making.

Our stories are fallen things too. Most storytellers don't see their work as a sacred act. Many don't acknowledge the Creator, much less recognize the echo of Him in their own faulty creations. And even when they do, their stories are often little more than warped reflections of God's own beautiful stories—the equivalent of a child's crayon drawing of a tree when one compares it with the awesome complexity of a live oak.

No writer, no matter how gifted or devout, can craft a *perfect* story. No movie director, no matter how talented and

God-honoring, can make a perfect movie. Whatever good we try to make falls short when measured against God's good artistry. That's just the way things are.

Genesis 1 and 2 give us the story of our creation and the story of our fall, and that leaves us with two important truths when it comes to the stories we, in turn, create.

First, few stories are wholly worthless. They are, after all, a mimicry of God's creative impulse, made by God's crowning creations. Just as our own worst sins are corruptions of God's gifts to us, a glimmer of God's goodness can be found in the folds of most of our stories if we look for them. I've called them God's fingerprints—hints, echoes of the glorious story He's been telling us throughout time.

Second, all stories are inevitably twisted creations too—made by sinners and tainted with sin. The stories we watch or read or play through are, in short, a lot like us: complex contradictions of good and bad. Sometimes lofty ideals mingle with tawdry inclinations; the better angels of our nature rubbing elbows with our inner demons.

And that's where *Plugged In* comes in.

FAILED TALES?

When I started working at *Plugged In*, one of my editors was Bob Smithouser. He ran the *Plugged In* podcast at the time, and he always signed off each episode with this snappy little tag: "It's not just entertainment."

Bob was absolutely right. It isn't.

Yes, we turn to movies to escape and relax. Many of us mindlessly watch television to decompress after a day at work or school. Entertainment is supposed to be, well, *entertaining*. We're not supposed to think too deeply about it, are we?

But think about what we've just gone over. We learn from the stories we're told—be they on paper or screen. We're programmed, by our very own creator, to not just learn from them but to love them as well. And while most every human story has a hint of God's creative impulse, it is also a product of our fallen world and its broken storytellers.

When we engage with the stories that our culture gives us, we're just following the design God gave us. God's design makes these stories incredibly influential—even when we don't think we're being influenced at all.

And the younger we are, the more likely it is that those stories will influence us. Kids may always worry about the monsters under their beds, but show them a horror movie featuring such a monster? Well, they just might be sleeping in *your* bed till they're twenty-seven!

Kids will always have some interest in sex. Expose a fourteen-year-old to an R-rated sex comedy, and what he sees on that screen may impact his relationships well into adulthood.

Studies show that kids who see smoking in movies are more likely to smoke. Kids who watch movies with a lot of swearing are more likely to swear themselves.

But that influence can go in a more positive direction too. What we see and hear and even play can move us in profound ways. We can learn. We can look at issues through a different set of eyes, feel compassion for people we've never met. Our stories can help us think and feel and grow. They can even help us think about God.

And often, we see those positives and negatives walk together, hand in hand, in our entertainment. Crass comedies can have a surprisingly tender heart. Profound dramas can be profane.

At *Plugged In*, we shuffle through it all—the good and the bad—to help you decide what's a good fit for you and your family. To decide, for yourselves, whether the gold you might find in the mud is worth digging out of that mud. So it's not for *us* to say whether a movie is worth seeing. It's for *you* to say. We just try to give you the information you need to make that decision on your own.

And so, yes, we count swear words. For some, one misuse of Jesus' name is enough to bar a movie from their family's watch list, whereas their Christian neighbor might choose to see the same movie, believing that the story has value overall and that the unfortunate language is an opportunity to discuss the issue of respecting God's name. Other families may be more sensitive to other words. For some mature viewers, two f-bombs might be navigable. But two hundred? Not so much.

If you haven't thought about entertainment like this before—or you haven't thought quite so deeply about it— well, you're in for a ride. A *fun* ride, I hope. For all its oddities, we love our job, and we hope you'll get a hint of that love as the book rolls on. But we feel it's an important job too— one that'll take you to a destination you and your family *need* to find: to understand why stories are so important and how you can sift them with care and wisdom. We'll teach you how to think about entertainment the way a *Plugged In* reviewer does. And we'll help you take those lessons and apply them to you and your children.

After all, it's not just entertainment.

PAW PRINTS

I was eight years old. The dentist told me I had a small mouth and too many teeth. So he pulled four of them—and gave me nine shots of Novocain to make sure I wouldn't feel a thing.

Until I got home. The numbness was wearing off, but I was still drooling all over myself. And slowly, the pain began to seep into my brain. I was miserable. Worse yet, I knew this was just the beginning. It was going to be a long night.

But when my dad came home from work, he was carrying an extravagant gift for our budget-conscious family: a box set of C. S. Lewis's Chronicles of Narnia books.

It took me about five days to read all seven of them. And for the next several years, I read through the series again and again. I laughed at Uncle Andrew in *The Magician's Nephew*. I literally cried during *The Last Battle*. One day I went outside and pushed aside the bushes in our backyard hoping to find a secret door or hole or train that might whisk me away to this imaginary place where I might meet Aslan, the Great Lion, the son of the Emperor-over-the-Sea, the King above all kings.

My favorite Aslan-related passage came from *The Horse and His Boy*. In it, Shasta—the boy from the title—has gotten separated from his party, and he's riding his horse alone in the mist. Only he's not really alone: Slowly he becomes aware of a *thing* walking next to him. And when he learns that it's a lion, he's naturally terrified. But as he and the lion talk (for the lion does talk), Shasta begins to understand that this is no ordinary lion; this lion is beyond comprehension, the source of all love and wisdom and light. And then—shortly after Shasta sees and understands fully the power that has been with him not just while walking in the mist but throughout his life as well—Aslan vanishes.

> "Was it all a dream?" wondered Shasta. But it couldn't have been a dream for there in the grass before him he saw the deep, large print of the Lion's front right paw. It took one's breath away to think of the weight that could make a footprint like that. But there was something more remarkable than the size about it. As he looked at it, water had already filled the bottom of it. Soon it was full to the brim, and then overflowing, and a little stream was running downhill, past him, over the grass.[2]

I set those books aside eventually. Indeed, I stopped reading altogether. The sixteen-year-old me had other interests, other things to do. And over the next several years, my faith started slipping too. It, like Narnia, seemed so important in my childhood. In college, it seemed less so.

Perhaps even childish.

But as I walked further from God, Aslan stayed with me. I recalled snippets from those books I'd read so often and loved so much. Like Shasta, I was lost in the mist of my own sorrows and cynicism. And eventually I, like Shasta, knew that despite it all, God was with me still—in the fog, listening and loving.

How powerful are stories? How can they change us?

Just ask me—the guy who has a map of Narnia on his bedroom wall. The guy who looks for God's fingerprints in this clouded, shrouded culture, including in our own fractured stories.

Let my colleagues and I at *Plugged In* show you what we see in the mist. Let's take a walk.

PART 1

Why It Matters

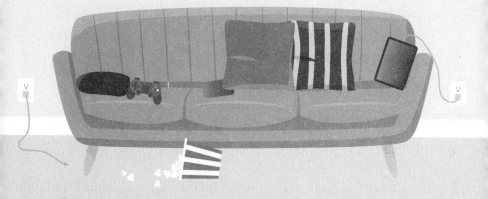

Remote

Adam R. Holz

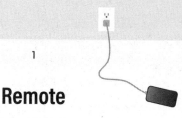

MY WIFE AND I ARE WATCHING the Denver Broncos on television. They're losing. Of course.

Still, they have plenty of time to make a comeback. The offense could get in a groove. The defense could force a turnover. The coach could fire his staff and—

Blip.

The TV switches to the Hallmark Channel, blissfully airing *Holiday Homecoming in Maple County*. Or something.

Has the television itself decided that the game is a lost cause? Has it detected my rising blood pressure and decided that I can stand to watch something a bit more . . . calming?

No. Televisions are getting more technologically savvy all the time, but they're not quite *that* advanced. (Yet.)

The real culprit is my wife, now holding the remote and gently smiling at the screen.

"What are you doing?" I ask her—not exactly matching the tranquility of the Hallmark Channel.

"Relax," she says. "It's a commercial. Just let me watch this a minute."

This is not the first time my wife has done this during a Broncos game. It is not even the first time she's done it during *this* Broncos game. But the contest is now hanging in the balance. And after thirty-nine seconds of watching it snow in Maple County, I snatch the remote, flip the channel back, and see . . . a car commercial.

"Argh," I growl. My wife looks at me.

"I just don't want to miss any of the game!" I desperately say.

She's still looking at me. It's the look a Jedi Master might give a foolish Padawan. It's a look that says, *I know when the game will be back on. We have another 94.6 seconds.*

She grabs the remote. Flicks back to an image of a pretty girl standing in the snow, looking at her hometown, wondering if perhaps life here is better than in the big city after all.

I start to sweat. The seconds tick by, agonizingly, interminably. I wonder if perhaps we've scored again. Or, more likely, thrown another interception.

She looks at me. *Calm down,* her eyes say. And in a few more moments, she clicks back to the game—a miraculous-but-maddening *two seconds* before the game resumes.

How does she do *that?* I wonder. If feels as if she must have made some Faustian bargain with the TV commercial deities, that she knows intuitively, almost magically, when the game will be back on.

We've been married nearly seventeen years now. This little scene has been repeated more times than I care to count. Yet still our little battle over the TV's remote control continues.

Who controls the remote? It's a marriage cliché, of course, the never-ending quest to wield the "one remote of power," thus controlling which images and stories flicker on our flat-screen TV. We're hardly the first couple to fight this battle. And, in truth, it's hardly a battle in my house anymore. I realized years ago that I wasn't likely to change my wife's predilection for channel surfing. But I do sometimes whine, "Can't we just leave it on one channel?" And every now and then, when I just can't stand it anymore, I grab the remote. I want the controller. I want *control*.

If at times there is conflict between spouses over this issue, however, it's nothing compared to the conflicts and concerns connected to our kids' use of screens and how they engage with all manner of entertainment through these pixilated windows. Trying to guide our children's relationships with screens is a potential minefield that's grown ever more complex in the advent of the information age, and especially since the proliferation of smartphones began around the year 2010 or so.

So what we're left with is, in a sense, a much *bigger* metaphorical battle about who controls the remote when it comes to our families' entertainment choices. And it's a battle with much bigger consequences than potentially missing a play or two of the big game if your spouse lingers a bit too long for comfort on the Hallmark Channel.

IT'S A SCREEN, SCREEN, SCREENED WORLD

Experts in the areas of pediatrics and child development usually suggest a two-hour-per-day screen-time limit for children—a subject we'll return to later in the book. Now, in the abstract, that might actually seem like a fairly generous allotment of time. But the reality is that too many kids spend much more than two hours a day in front of a screen. The 2019 Common Sense Census tells us that eight-to-twelve-year-old kids engage with screens an average of four hours and forty-four minutes a day, while the average teen is on for seven hours and twenty-two minutes. And that's not including homework or school-related screen usage.[1] (Common Sense Media updates this survey every few years, and the trends in screen time, not surprisingly, have gone only one direction in the past fifteen years: up.)

Obviously, there's a huge gap between what experts recommend and what our kids are actually doing with screens. And during the coronavirus pandemic, researchers suggested that screen-time usage (particularly among older kids with access to personal devices) was 52 percent higher than in pre-pandemic times.[2] One study went so far as saying that adults spent a whopping *seventeen hours a day* on their screens during the coronavirus—which, if extrapolated to a full lifetime, would translate to *forty-four years*.[3] Clearly this isn't just a problem for tweens and teens.

Our instinctive response as parents when we feel that our kids' screen engagement is out of whack is to (figuratively) grab the remote and change the channel. Certainly, established boundaries for what our kids see on-screen and how much time they spend there are an important part of the equation, and we'll talk about those, too.

But given the proliferation of screens in our lives and the lives of our kids, we as parents need more than just drill-sergeant commands to limit how our children interact with entertainment. And our kids need more than that too. We must understand more deeply *how* the ideas they're interacting with are shaping them. We also need to cultivate an *active, engaged, and intentional* stance in how we relate to our devices—instead of a passive, consumeristic one.

Perhaps most importantly, we need a vision of what we want the outcome for our children to be as they mature and eventually launch into young adulthood themselves.

WHEN OUR KIDS ARE "REMOTE"

As our children move through the teen years, they'll increasingly be asking for more control. How do we respond? How do we help shape their hearts and souls for the quickly approaching season when we as parents no longer have our hands on that proverbial remote control?

Just as every couple has likely argued over who gets to operate the remote control, every one of us as parents has also had to navigate the first experience of learning that our son or daughter has been exposed to something we wish they hadn't—thus facing the sobering realization that parental control is more limited than we had hoped. And despite our best intentions to protect our kids, at some point that will happen to all of us—whether our children tell us about it or not.

When my son was around six or seven years old, he went to a friend's house for the afternoon. When he got back, he was raving about a video game they'd played with his friend's dad, who was in the armed services. The game? One of the *Call of Duty* series titles.

Now, if you know anything about video games, you probably understand why alarm bells went off in my head. "You played *what*?!" I was tempted to say. After all, this franchise is rated M (for "mature" audiences, seventeen years old or older) for brutally realistic combat and harsh profanity.

But the fact of the matter was that it had already happened, and there was nothing I could do to undo it. What I *could* do, however, was ask him about the game, listen to his responses, and try to help him understand why we wouldn't be playing that game in our house (which he definitely wanted to do).

Boundaries Breached

When my son was fourteen, someone sent him an unsolicited, inappropriate picture via his Google Hangouts account. My two daughters found it first, since they were using our laptop for a school assignment.

"Um, Dad, you'd better come look at this," they said.

Now, my daughters have a penchant for drama and never miss a chance to get their older brother in trouble. But I wasn't prepared for the image I saw when I walked over to the computer. I wasn't prepared for feeling like my children's innocence had all been sullied in that moment.

My wife and I spent the next three hours talking through what we'd seen with all three of our children. It was an unwanted, unasked-for image, to be sure—but *there it was.* And now it was important that we talked about it.

"Why would anyone send a picture like that?" one of them asked in tears, genuinely bewildered.

It was a good question. And despite my anger and frustration in that moment, it proved to be an excellent opportunity to talk about some hard-but-important issues that almost all families today will have to deal with at some point. (Later in the book, we'll be talking more about the reality of sexting, as this phenomenon is called.)

Remote...but Controlled

As parents, we're tempted to try to create a hermetically sealed environment that we can control completely, monitoring everything that comes in and out of our children's lives. As you've seen in my own story, that doesn't always work.

But even as we work diligently to protect our kids from threats that we can and should minimize, we must keep the end goal in mind: gradually granting them increasing freedom to make their own decisions as they move through adolescence but modeling discernment, communication, and wisdom as we go.

When our children spread their wings and leave our homes as young adults, what do we want for them in the areas of entertainment, technology, and discernment? We want them to be able to think critically and biblically about their entertainment choices and technology usage. Achieving that goal requires a strategy that both shields them from destructive content and gradually moves them into dialoguing about content and worldview as they grow into their middle-teen years.

The result? By the time our children are remote from us physically and relationally, they'll have learned what it looks like to exercise control in their media, entertainment, and technology choices. Leaving the nest won't be as much an opportunity to go crazy trying all the stuff Mom and Dad wouldn't let them do as it will be the next step in their development. At that point, they will already have practiced making entertainment and technology choices on their own—with our guidance and active engagement.

ENGAGED, BUT NOT PERFECT

Our hope is that this book will provide you, as parents, with a practical, relational, and theologically grounded road map to help you and your children wisely navigate the screen-saturated world in which we live.

As you've probably noticed by now, our *Plugged In* team isn't writing about this topic from an ivory tower. We're sharing our own experiences and hard-learned lessons from the perspectives of sons and daughters, mothers and fathers, and media users ourselves. We're all navigating the very things we discuss in this book. Sometimes we get things right and our kids make great decisions. Other times, maybe not. You'll see both successes and failures in the pages that follow.

Our desire is not to paint an unrealistically rosy or overly formulaic portrait of parenting in a screen-saturated culture.

Rather, we hope to come alongside you and offer specific, concrete, and hard-won wisdom about what may be the most influential issue families face today: dealing with the proliferation of screens and the content that can come with them.

Rather than advocating perfection, we'd like to lay before you this goal as fellow parents: consistent, intentional engagement with our kids and with the reality of how screens influence their lives today. As we set limits, ask questions, and thoughtfully discuss choices and the areas where we've set limits, we'll model an ongoing and critical conversation about entertainment and media, not just saying "Because I said so" to our children and shutting them down.

As a dad of three, I'm deeply aware of my own failings and inconsistencies. I don't always get it right—a fact I'm sure my children would agree with if I invited them to chime in here. That said, my wife and I *are* seeking to raise our three kids by the principles and ideas, goals and desires you'll read about in this book.

GROWING IN BIBLICAL MEDIA DISCERNMENT

One of the ideas we'll be talking about a lot in this book is *media discernment.* You may already know exactly what I mean by that phrase. But if not, I want to flesh it out a bit before we move into the meat of this book.

In a nutshell, exercising biblical media discernment involves comparing the on-screen content we encounter with what we find in Scripture. Over and over in the Bible, we read about how our faith compels and propels us to live differently from the world in terms of our perspectives and behaviors.

In the book of Ephesians, for instance, the apostle Paul spends the first three chapters of his letter helping us understand how our relationship with Jesus transforms us from the inside out, giving us a new identity and a new sense of purpose and calling in our lives. In fact, it's hard to pull out just one passage to illustrate that point, since one gets the sense that Paul was barely able to take a breath as he wrote this letter to the church at Ephesus:

> [God] chose us in [Christ] before the creation of the world to be holy and blameless in his sight. In love he predestined us for adoption to sonship through Jesus Christ, in accordance with his pleasure and will—to the praise of his glorious grace, which he has freely given us in the One he loves. In him we have redemption through his blood, the forgiveness of sins, in accordance with the riches of God's grace that he lavished on us. With all wisdom and understanding, he made known to us the mystery of his will according to his good pleasure, which he purposed in Christ, to be put into effect when the times reach their fulfillment—to bring unity to all things in heaven and on earth under Christ.
>
> EPHESIANS 1:4-10

EMBRACING OUR CALLING AND IDENTITY IN CHRIST

For Paul, the conversation about our calling and identity begins and ends with a profound sense of how Jesus' sacrifice changes us from the inside out. Our identity and calling are shaped and defined by Jesus' death on our behalf and our embrace of what His gift graciously offers us.

That calling and identity utterly revolutionize the way we see the world, such that we no longer passively or mindlessly accept ideas or ways of life that the world wouldn't give a second thought to. Instead, Paul urges us to "live a life worthy of the calling you have received" (Ephesians 4:1), to make choices in keeping with our identity as children of God whom Jesus paid the ultimate price to save.

To exercise biblical media discernment, then, is to compare our entertainment choices with what Scripture says is true, noble, right, pure, lovely, admirable, excellent, and praiseworthy (Philippians 4:8). When we engage with entertainment and technology through this grid, it changes our perspective on both *what* movies and TV shows we watch and *how* we watch them, on how we interact with online content, and on what entertainment choices we're willing to make.

This kind of media discernment is something we should practice as parents, even as we model it and teach our children how to do the same. And *that* requires one more important step: critiquing the seductive notion that the entertainment we choose doesn't really matter.

MOVING BEYOND "NEUTRAL-ZONE" THINKING

It's tempting—very tempting, actually—to indulge the notion that we can dabble in stories and entertainment with big content and worldview issues and not be influenced or shaped by them. Sure, we might stay away from the "really bad" stuff. But like the proverbial frog in the kettle, we can easily minimize entertainment's potentially problematic influence because we just don't realize how hot the water has gotten.

I call this *neutral-zone thinking*.

History is filled with plenty of neutral zones. But when I think of *the* Neutral Zone, I think of the universe of *Star Trek*. According to StarTrek.com, the Neutral Zone is "an area of space between the United Federation of Planets and the Romulan Star Empire that measures approximately one light year and serves as a 'buffer' zone. Any incursion into the Romulan Neutral Zone is considered a hostile act."[4] And anyone who has watched *Star Trek* knows just how hostile that act could get.

If you prefer to think in more real-world terms, the neutral zone is a lot like the demilitarized zone between North and South Korea. It's a place where two warring powers agree not to go, a "safe space" of sorts between them.

Now, you might be thinking, *What on earth (or in space!) does this have to do with technology and the entertainment media that flows through it?* Great question! I'm glad you asked.

As Christians and even as parents, we can drift passively, almost unconsciously, into neutral-zone thinking when it comes to the bombardment of media and technology we face today.

We know the "big" things we want to help our kids avoid, such as pornography, graphic violence, and sexual entertainment. We recognize that these things are at war with the convictions we hold as Christ followers. But when it comes to the "little" things, well, we can almost unconsciously treat them as if they're *neutral*, when in fact they might very well be communicating subtle messages and worldviews that are very much at odds with our Christian faith.

The apostle Paul repeatedly challenged the mentality of neutral-zone thinking in the book of Ephesians (though, of course, he didn't actually have Romulans in mind!): "Be very careful, then, how you live—not as unwise but as wise, making the most of every opportunity, because the days are evil. Therefore do not be foolish, but understand what the Lord's will is" (Ephesians 5:15-17).

Paul understood that the culture influences how we live. So he tells us to "pay attention," a phrase that the King James Version translates "walk circumspectly" (verse 15). In other words, don't just mindlessly absorb and consume what you're walking through. Instead, look up, look around, and be aware of the influences that seek to shape your heart and mind in ways that are at odds with a biblical faith and worldview.

This is not a casual suggestion from Paul, who went on to say that "the days are evil" (verse 16). If we're not paying attention and seeking to "understand what the Lord's will is," he tells us, we risk being sucked into the gravitational pull of a worldly way of life that's opposed to the gospel (see verse 18). He reiterates the same idea in Romans 12:2: "Do not conform to the pattern of this world, but be transformed by the renewing of your mind. Then you will be able to test and approve what God's will is—his good, pleasing and perfect will." The contrast here is clear: being shaped by the world or being transformed by truth as we walk with God.

It's critical, obviously, to understand what's happening in the world of technology and media influence if we hope to limit and counterbalance potentially harmful influences in those arenas—which is exactly what my *Plugged In* colleagues and I hope to accomplish in the chapters that follow.

We Get Only One Brain

Danny Huerta

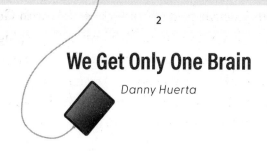

"I HATE MY PARENTS!" the teen boy told me.

"Why do you hate your parents?" I asked.

"Because they disconnected my Xbox and hid the cord!" he said.

"Why would they do that?"

"They said that I've been angry all the time, and that I'm not getting anything done, and that I'm spending too much time on video games. But that's not true! Besides, all my friends are online! My parents are taking away my only outlet, and it's so dumb!"

As a family counselor, I've heard several variations of this story. While entertainment has been a pain point for families ever since the first movie flickered on the first screen, conflicts surrounding entertainment and technology have grown exponentially in the last few decades. In recent years, I've heard about countless family conversations concerning video games, social media and smartphones, and internet access, as well as many other entertainment outlets. As if raising kids wasn't hard enough, technology and entertainment have made things even more complicated for parents, especially intentional Christian parents.

Those parents are truly engaged in a battle, waging war over the precious real estate of their children's minds. And the stakes couldn't be higher. As we'll see in this chapter, what your sons and daughters engage in—be it movies or music, TikTok or YouTube, or any of the other legions of outlets that fall under the entertainment and technology umbrella—impacts their brains and souls deeply. When you're dealing with young minds, which are absorbing information and changing quickly anyway, the influence of entertainment is that much more powerful—and that much more dangerous.

Parents need to be aware of these influences and understand how and why they are so impactful, particularly on a young person's brain. But in the midst of this battle, there's hope: You can provide a foundational example for your children by thoughtfully managing your own brain's "real estate" and by patiently and diligently guiding your kids as they manage theirs.

HOOKS

Have you ever wondered what a fish thinks about when it bites into what seems like an incredible meal but finds instead a painful metal hook? I sometimes imagine that fish with a thought bubble above its head: *Oh no! I wish someone had warned me about these painful and deadly things floating in the water. They really hurt!*

Do fish ever learn? In catch-and-release bodies of water, are fish just a bit more cautious after they've been caught and thrown back into the water for another chance to live? Or do they fall for the same bait over and over until finally they wind up on somebody's dinner table? Well, since they're not all that smart, fish do indeed fall for the same free-food scam again and again. I picture that fish considering another meal dangling in front of its googly eyes with another thought bubble above its head: *This seems really familiar, but I think it's different this time. I'll get a little closer and maybe just see.*

Sometimes humans aren't all that different. We may be able to remember dangers far longer than your average fish. We may be able to understand concepts like long division, while your average fish doesn't even understand concepts like water or dry land. But similar hooks in our own lives catch us time after time.

The truth is that thousands of inviting lures compete for our attention while we try to attend to our day-to-day demands. From the time we wake up to the moment we close our eyes to sleep, we're bombarded with stimuli that our brains try to process and respond to effectively. Corporate interests—from coders and cinematic storytellers to social media CEOs and advertising executives—not only add to all that stimuli but also manipulate our responses to favor their interests.

These stimuli are ultimately like candy for the brain. And, like sugar, the more we consume, the more we crave. We're hooked on the communication, information, entertainment, and gratification that technology has to offer. Most people never realize they're hooked, which leads to an ever-growing dependence on these artificial sources of fulfillment. Others recognize the hook and try to break free of it through digital fasts and short-lived commitments to new limitations. But when the next appealing bit of bait comes along, all too often they forget how hard it was to get rid of the hook, and they take another bite. And once again, they're hooked.

The stimuli available on modern personal technology have been carefully engineered to create an immersive experience that we have a difficult time disconnecting from. Humans have gone from being passive listeners of radio to passive watchers of television to fully immersed consumers of multimedia entertainment. This more immersive environment can have powerful effects on the brain. Game designers make sure we have a hard time putting down the controller. TV streamers encourage us to binge hours of shows at a time. Social media designers encourage us to scroll endlessly through our feeds.

In other words, it's all by design. But how did they do it?

HOW THE BRAIN IS WIRED

In a way, the old adage *The more you own, the more it owns you* describes the impact of digital devices on people today. Given the amount of time and attention our devices pull from us, you might say our devices *own* us. Walking around town, you'll notice many people's eyes glued to some kind of screen. Modern society is now so dependent on technology and digital devices that it cannot escape the complications and challenges that come with their impact on the brain and relationships.

As a family counselor, I know that when young people come to my office, it's because the adults in their lives—moms, dads, teachers, guardians—are concerned about them. They might be worried about the young person's schoolwork or how they're behaving at home or in public. But behavior is really only a symptom of the real issue. So to understand what's happening, other areas must be considered, including their family and home experience and their relationships within and outside the family. Even genetics can play a part here. The real problem is not the troublesome behavior but something within the bigger picture of their lives that may be fueling that behavior.

One source that fuels problematic behaviors among kids today is the many messages and temptations that arise from technology use and the consumption of entertainment. All too often, these influences lead young people down harmful and destructive paths.

Sometimes kids are savvy enough to recognize the power that media and technology have over them, and they may even initiate change themselves. I'll never forget the time my son came to me and said, "Dad, can you put limits on my Nintendo DS?" He explained that it was taking up too much of his time, and he had even noticed some changes in how he was acting toward us.

It was exciting for my wife and me to see our son learning to manage his internal world, but his desire for control over his tech use didn't appear out of a vacuum. As parents, we had been very intentional in talking with our kids about the powerful impacts of digital devices on their brains. We had also given our son many limits, and he had earned more freedoms as he'd gained our trust. Like many kids, he abused that trust at times, such as sneaking his DS into the bathroom and spending hours on the toilet playing video games. He was also dishonest with us about the amount of time he was spending on it. But I think he was in a good position to recognize the dangerous hooks underneath the entertaining bait because we had put limits on his DS use and explained *why* they were important. We didn't simply lock down his device and announce, "Because I say so." Because he understood the *why* behind our actions, he also understood that he wasn't hurting us when he violated the limits on his DS. He was hurting himself. Even though he was disobeying us and disregarding the rules we had put in place, they still meant something to him.

Of our two children, our son is the one who has been naturally drawn to screens since he was a toddler. We'd often laugh over the fact that he would be instantly mesmerized by television screens at restaurants.

But he's hardly alone. Most of us are drawn to screens and the entertainment or experiences they offer us. As mentioned earlier, technology and entertainment companies recognize this attraction and exploit it. They understand that human brains are wired a certain way, and they can engineer their products to ever more effectively capture our attention.

Dopamine

The more media and technology we consume, the more our brains anticipate a rewarding experience. A quick surge of dopamine is released in response to what happens on a screen—whether we're watching a movie, shopping online for shoes, or reading interesting information. Dopamine is a chemical our bodies make and our nervous systems use to send messages around the brain and body. This chemical messenger, or neurotransmitter, plays a big role in the human body's ability to think and plan. It's also a big part of how we experience pleasure. When we see something interesting or do something exciting, we get a dopamine boost. We even get a boost when we anticipate a rewarding experience. But there's always a little crash afterward—and a constant craving to get another boost. That's why we're able to mindlessly scroll through social media or binge TV shows without hitting the pause button. We're seeking more of the high to escape the lows of our stressful world.[1]

Several years ago, a teenage boy came to my practice for help. He was struggling with anxiety and depression, but he also had a gaming addiction. Whenever he spent less time playing video games, he would experience an increase in anxiety, but his depression would decrease. We explored healthy strategies and tools to manage his anxious feelings, and these were helpful for a time, but they could not compete with the dopamine-oozing experience of gaming. When he went to college in another state, he became addicted to video games once again—only this time, his addiction became even stronger. He would play games for more than eight hours each day. As an adult, he returned to my office for help. He said he was struggling with deep depression and overwhelming anxiety while trying to maintain a job and navigate his addiction.

Video games enable players to live out their fantasies, from exploring strange worlds to driving exotic cars to competing on the highest (virtual) sports stages imaginable. For many players, gaming is just an enjoyable pastime to decompress away from real-world stresses. But for others, the games themselves become their "real" world—thanks to the manipulations of their designers—or at least a world preferable to the one they're actually living in. For my client, everyday life couldn't compete with the flood of dopamine he got from playing video games.

When dopamine levels increase, the brain remembers a specific experience and is motivated to have that experience again and again. In a way, the brain bookmarks the experience as a place it wants to return to repeatedly.

In fact, scientists have discovered that devices increase dopamine to the same extent that sex and drugs like cocaine do. In other words, screens have the capacity to create an extremely stimulating and addictive response. Dr. Peter Whybrow, former director of the Semel Institute for Neuroscience and Human Behavior at UCLA, has described screens and video games as "electronic cocaine."[2] Dr. Andrew Doan, head of addiction research for the US Navy in 2016, compared screen time to "digital *pharmakeia*" (the Greek term for "drugs" that forms the root of our English word *pharmaceuticals*).[3] Chinese teachers and parents have described internet addiction as "electronic heroin" or "electronic opium."[4] And an addiction therapist from England observed that giving smartphones to our children is like giving them a full "gram of cocaine" because of how damaging and addictive it can be.[5]

No wonder many tech executives are reluctant to let their own children use the digital drugs they've created. Apple's Steve Jobs once told *The New York Times* that he didn't allow his kids to use iPads. "We limit how much technology our kids use at home," he said. The same article reported that several other technology CEOs and venture capitalists also placed strict limits on their children's screen time.[6]

These individuals understood how their technological creations hooked users. Those shiny devices with their glowing screens cause us to hunger for more and more digital content. Yet the more we binge something, the less enjoyable it is, and the more dopamine boosts we seek. In other words, we'll look for more, bigger, better, and faster when it comes to dopamine-inducing experiences. That's true of all of us, but it's especially true during the teen years, when brains are changing and growing so rapidly. As the brain learns to anticipate pleasure from screens, it releases a dopamine hit similar to when we anticipate sex, a vacation, or an incredible dessert.

And our screens aren't just bombarding us with dopamine hits. They're changing us in other ways too—even when we're not doing anything at all.

Sleep Deprivation

As we consider behaviors that impact the brain, we must also recognize that sleep is necessary for a healthy brain. The brain is (obviously) part of the human body, and a body that doesn't rest has big problems. Even the best athletes will break down if they're never given a chance to rest and heal. The brain operates the same way. If we don't get enough sleep, our brains won't operate like they should—and neither will we.

Sleep deprivation can lead to big problems, including mental-health issues, poor memory, reckless decision making, and increased levels of anxiety, moodiness, and depression.[7]

Interestingly, the overuse of technology and the lure of screens, especially late at night, can actually deplete our dopamine neurotransmitters and cause sleep deprivation. A lack of sleep combined with using digital devices all day creates a perfect storm for the brain, depleting our ability to exercise self-control. When we're tired, it's much more difficult to say no to the next click, scroll, or video game that is designed to create constant yeses in our brains. What does that do to a young child trying to develop self-control?

Attention and Imitation

If the one-two punch of screens and dopamine can mess with our sleep, you might imagine the influence they have on us when we're awake and fully engaged.

Screen use specializes in delivering quick hits of dopamine: You see a video you like, and you get a rush of the neurotransmitter. But that encourages you to seek out more and more videos—and the shorter the better. It's one of the reasons TikTok is so addictive for kids (and adults) and actually shortens their attention spans. With the average video just fifteen seconds long and a never-ending supply of clips pushed into the user's scroll, it's a constant source of dopamine.[8]

Personal devices have whittled down attention spans, too, especially in children. Brains get used to those rapid-fire dopamine hits. Without them, our brains get bored and eager to move on to something else. With shorter attention spans, we spend more time using the limbic region of our brains (where our emotional and behavioral responses live) without input from the more rational prefrontal cortex, which requires more energy and time to engage and influence decision making. Like a child returning to a candy dish, we return for more dopamine-triggering stimulation, pushing away the less immediately rewarding disciplines of thought, consideration, and discernment.[9]

Interestingly, in the last twenty years or so, a new field has emerged that fuses traditional business tactics with brain science. Called *neuromarketing*, the neuroscientists and marketers who work in this field have a clear goal: to capture our attention and emotions so we'll purchase certain products or services. Neuromarketing uses neuroscience, marketing, and technology to create loyal followers and repeat consumers—essentially manipulating the way our brains work in order to make a profit.[10]

Of course, this sort of manipulation is nothing new. Visual storytellers and marketers have had similar goals for nearly a century—well before they knew exactly how their work influenced the brains of viewers and customers. This influence involves something called *mirror neurons*, which scientists have been researching for more than three decades. Neurons are types of cells in the brain that send and receive messages from rest of the body, and mirror neurons perform a couple of useful functions. First, they help us learn from and copy other people's movements, such as studying NBA star Stephen Curry's jump shot to see how it might help young players improve their own basketball performances. Mirror neurons also enable us to feel empathy and compassion for others by allowing us, in a way, to step into someone else's shoes. When we watch YouTube videos, television programs, or movies, our mirror neurons are activated, and we experience events almost as if we are participating in them ourselves. In other words, the person watching the screen has a mental experience quite similar to what the person in the actual situation would be experiencing. What an escape from reality! All these forms of entertainment can be interesting as well as distressing.

You've likely felt the impact of your own mirror neurons. Consider how you feel when a basketball player for your favorite team is shooting free throws to win the game, or when the quarterback of your favorite football team is starting a game-clinching drive: Your heart rate goes up, and you might start breathing faster. Part of you feels as if you're on the court or on the field with them.

Consider how you feel when characters in a scary movie start creeping into that dark, cold basement. Or when a couple in a rom-com holds hands for the first time. Or when a beloved character in a TV series dies. You're not just watching these things happen. In a way, you're living these things along with the characters.[11] Other forms of media play on this dynamic as well. Books draw you into worlds that feel almost real—even though they're nothing but black-and-white words on a page. Video games take you into the action on a whole different level.

So mirror neurons can make the entertainment we engage with all the more powerful. But they can also come with some powerfully negative consequences. Pornography, for example, is so addictive because users' brains partly perceive that the person or people they're watching are performing for them—as if they were there in person. It takes sex, one of God's greatest creations, and twists it, turning it from an act of deep intimacy into a false, artificial connection. And because that connection is so seductive and addictive, people will do almost anything to justify it. A survey published by Statista revealed that 43 percent of people think pornography is morally acceptable—evidence that the brain can be duped.[12]

The brain will react the way it is designed to react. These reactions aren't bad in and of themselves. We're made this way to better connect to each other. But the ability and desire to connect also makes our brains susceptible to manipulation by people who know how the brain works and use high-tech tools and tactics to trick us into embracing whatever they're peddling.

Yet even if our brains are vulnerable, our minds are under our control. Yes, the mind is a part of the brain, but it's also set apart from the raw reactions the brain is susceptible to. The mind is more than the information the brain receives and processes over time. Our minds encompass our experiences and our perceptions of those experiences, what we've learned, what we want, and the decisions we make along the way. I like to imagine the brain as a kind of mailbox, where all sorts of information and stimuli are gathered, and the mind as the more intentional part of us that decides what to keep and what to throw away. We learn how to sift all that information through time and experience. We get to build and guard our minds. They are the real estate we get to manage, navigate, and direct. In other words, the mind is what we manage in response to what is happening in our brains, our relationships, and our experiences. When our brains experience boredom or stimulation or curiosity, our minds tell us what to do with it. When our brains tell us that we should eat another five cookies, our minds tell us *Not so fast.*

I have said something like this to countless clients in my counseling practice: "You only get one brain, so use your mind to manage, build, guard, and grow a history you want to remember and a future you hope to experience. Protect your brain from its vulnerabilities by managing your mind with eyes wide open. That is the real estate that guards your soul, your relationships, and your identity—and it is under constant attack."

That's a message we need to hear as parents so we can help our children build and guard their minds as well.

HIJACKED HUMANS

Digital devices are intentionally designed to hijack the brain by exploiting four core developmental needs that God has designed in human nature: a sense of belonging and connection, a sense of worth, a sense of competence, and a sense of meaning and purpose. Let's unpack each one to see how technology co-opts our divine design for its own ends.

A Sense of Belonging and Connection

The first core human need that digital devices masterfully exploit is our need for belonging and connection. Marketers and creators of smartphones and social media promise more connection than ever before, but that promise is an illusion. An entire generation of people is deeply struggling with loneliness in spite of all their social media connections. In fact, loneliness has become a silent, underlying epidemic among teens and young adults. According to a national survey conducted in 2020, more than 60 percent of millennial and Gen Z adults reported feeling lonely.[13] Another survey found that 42 percent of millennial women fear loneliness more than a cancer diagnosis.[14]

All humans crave connection and belonging. Text messages and social media posts on digital devices can give the illusion of being connected but tend to leave users feeling empty and lonely. We can accumulate masses of online "friends" and yet have very few friends we can talk with face-to-face about deeper issues. Our brains are duped into thinking that we're connecting when we're really longing for deeper, trustworthy, real-life relationships.

Even when we do have face-to-face connections, the presence of technology can undermine opportunities to actually connect. One example is following multiple online conversations while we're talking to someone face-to-face.[15] When we do this, we're unable to feel a sense of connectedness and belonging in any one place.

That sort of disconnectedness isn't just unhealthy; it is also unbiblical. God's Word frequently reminds us that we are made to be in close relationship with God and with other believers. Scripture describes God's relationship with His people and a believer's relationship with others using the language of a close, connected family. We are God's children and have an eternal inheritance with Him. Fellow believers are our beloved brothers and sisters in Christ, and we are called to value true connection and real-world relationships (Hebrews 10:24-25).

God's Word reassures us that He loves us and welcomes us into His family. God says we already *belong*! What a different experience from the isolation and loneliness that technology often gives us.

A Sense of Worth

The second fundamental need that digital devices hijack is our sense of worth. Social media and video games are designed to give an illusion of worth that requires an endless investment of time pursuing it. Like someone lost in the desert thirsting for water, we thirst to feel known, and social media promises countless opportunities to share our lives with the world. We've all seen teens obsessing over their social media posts and poses while missing out on the real-world life that is happening right in front of them.

While the initial dopamine rush from online activity can give us a temporary sense of worth, the feelings quickly fade, leaving us with a craving for more. Trying to find our self-worth online is ultimately a futile pursuit. The "likes" we get from strangers or acquaintances inevitably feel empty. When we spend all our time and energy trying to earn approval in an online world, we're unable to enjoy living in the real world.

We know that seeking self-worth online can be damaging, but it can also be deadly. Research has shown that young adults who use social media on a regular basis are three times more likely to suffer from depression as individuals in the same age groups who generally avoid social media. This puts a significant number of young people at risk of suicide.[16]

On top of making us feel depressed, social media can make us feel worthless. We look at the perfect pictures of our perfect friends with their perfect accomplishments and perfect vacations, and we begin to wonder why we're not as happy or as good-looking or as successful as they are. We might even conclude that something is wrong with us. Instead of cultivating a sense of worth, social media aids and abets feelings of failure and worthlessness.

Jesus died on the cross so that we could become God's adopted children and live eternally with Him. Our sense of worth must come from recognizing that God loves us and sees us through a totally different lens. We are His beloved masterpieces, created to follow His beautiful plan for our lives (Ephesians 2:10). That is real worth!

A Sense of Competence

The third core human need that technology hijacks is our need to feel like we're good at something. The internet opens up a ton of exciting ways for young people to engage with the wider world through social media. Post a video online, and they can receive immediate feedback. That makes them want to post more videos and images, especially if they get a lot of positive hits. All this affirmation gives them a strong dopamine surge that creates a desire for even more.

In the world of video games, anyone can feel competent. Small, muscle-challenged individuals can become powerful warriors online. But this power can become an obsession, an escape from a reality that ultimately makes gamers feel powerless.

Like the young man I mentioned earlier, another young man came into my office irate at his parents for pulling the plug on his video games. He said, "I'm the best player in the world. This is crazy! Why would my parents do this?" He loved the affirmation he got from gaming, the sense of being powerful and respected. He felt known, feared, and highly skilled. But this imaginary world was ripping him away from his real life and responsibilities, in which he wasn't doing as well.

Social media and video games can give our kids (and users of any age!) a false sense of competence. Online, there are seemingly limitless possibilities to demonstrate abilities and receive immediate feedback. But it's devastating when young people realize that their successes in the real world just don't measure up to those in that fake one. They don't unlock new abilities or get high scores at school or work like they do online. Math tests or counseling sessions aren't as thrilling as fighting zombies and being flying dragons or getting lots of positive feedback from an Instagram post. Saying something funny in the lunchroom doesn't reward them with the "likes" they crave.

Modern technology has drawn us all into unrealistic worlds filled with unrealistic successes that give us an unrealistic sense of competence. We've lost the ability to appreciate the slower, quieter achievements that feed our real mental, emotional, and spiritual needs. We've stopped working to become competent in the real world because it seems much more satisfying to demonstrate our skills in false online worlds.

A Sense of Meaning and Purpose

The fourth core need that has been hijacked in our device-driven culture is a sense of meaning and purpose. Video games and social media provide users with a sort of hero's journey, a way to save the day and enjoy the admiration of others. Gamers can find meaning and purpose defeating the bad guys while teaming up with people from around the world.

Tech designers and marketers also hit gamers' brains with a one-two punch by connecting gaming with social media. This has become a lucrative environment for some gamers and television producers, but it baffles older generations, who used to find the most enjoyment from *playing* instead of watching others play.

Earning money while doing something fun on social media could feel like a meaningful pursuit. Humans thirst for purpose in life, and finding it can be quite exciting. But life isn't all about making money. Our brains can be tricked into thinking there is true meaning and purpose in an online world filled with slot-machine rewards.

What if we pursued Christ—our audience of one—to find our real purpose? God already gives our lives meaning. In His Kingdom we find belonging. In Him we have value and purpose and competence.

The more we pursue the illusions of the digital world and model this for our kids, the more this world captivates our brains, and the less room there is for Christ to captivate them. And the less the brain is captivated by Christ, the less likely it is that we (or our kids) will pursue a real and satisfying relationship with Him. Big challenges are on the horizon. The more tech developers and programmers learn about each of us, the more our interactions with entertainment and technology will be tailored to fit us, and the better technology will exploit our core needs, wants, and feelings. It will manipulate us and our children in ways we can't even imagine right now, using our memories, ideals, and worldviews to make its charms ever harder to resist.

Scary, huh?

MIND YOUR MINDS (AND THE NEGATIVE IMPACTS AROUND YOU)

"Daddy and Mommy, stop googling. I just want to talk!"

Tech obsession isn't just an issue for children and teens. Many parents struggle with screens just as much as their kids do. Our brains want more screens, more social media, more excitement, more dopamine hits. And our minds have a hard time telling our brains when it's time to quit. This conflict can dramatically affect the quality of parent-child relationships.

During one counseling session, a mom told me that she was desperate to get her son to cut down on his screen time. She was frustrated by the fact that he was "always on his phone, texting and posting on social media." To which the teen replied, "I'll stop once my mom stops texting while she's driving, which she does all the time. She is just as addicted to her phone as I am." It was a very awkward moment for that mom as she tried to stumble through a response.

This mom isn't alone. Many teens have shared with me their concerns regarding their parents' use of digital devices. And I'm not the only counselor who has heard such complaints. According to a recent survey by Common Sense Media, the majority of teens and parents agree that they spend too much time on their phones, and 28 percent of teens believe that their parents are "addicted" to their devices.[17]

Children and teens have told me their parents have a hard time putting down their phones at mealtime, in the car, and at night. On the other hand, many parents complain about their kids' addictions to video games, social media, or their smartphones.

Parents' use of digital devices to the point that it severely interferes with family communication and interaction is such a problem that scientists have come up with a name for it: *technoference*. Parental technoference can lead to serious health and behavior problems for children, including mental-health issues, such as depression and anxiety.[18]

Although personal technology and entertainment are here to stay, it does not mean that the battle is lost. In response to this reality, we're invited to be more aware and intentional in the ways we manage ourselves and guide our kids. We are responsible for what goes on in our homes, regardless of what the culture around us does. We get to pray, reflect on, and lead our families with wisdom as we navigate the interactions between our brains and the varieties of addictive brain candy clamoring for our attention.

THE ULTIMATE CONNECTION

As technology changes and grows, and as it becomes even more incorporated into how we learn, work, and live, its impacts will change and grow too. While some changes may be good, many future impacts will follow the negative, and even harmful, trends of the past and the present.

Technology by itself isn't bad. We all communicate through personal devices, and we all enjoy entertainment. But God didn't design us to stare at screens all day, pursuing an addictive, artificial world. He doesn't care whether you finish a game level or rack up a million views on your latest YouTube video. These roads don't lead to a sense of belonging and connection, worth, competence, or meaning and purpose.

God designed us to communicate differently. He made us to look each other in the eye and take each other by the hand. He loves it when we share our real lives with one another. He longs for us to *love* one another—not just click a thumbs-up button.

Most importantly, God wants us to never, ever lose sight of Him—the One who loves us most of all and makes our love for one another possible.

Scripture tells us to "set [our] minds on things above, not on earthly things" (Colossians 3:2). Why? Because that's where our true hope, our true satisfaction, and our true worth lie. Everything else is worthless chaff that blows away in the wind (Psalm 1:4).

Yet as we seek to set our minds on higher things or look for something better and brighter to believe in, our entertainment and technology can often lead us astray. That's what we'll be talking about in the next chapter.

3

Belief

Paul Asay

I WAS AROUND FIVE YEARS OLD when my best friend, Terry, insisted that Superman was real.

"Nu-*uh*," I said. (I was apparently already a cynic.)

"Yuh-*huh*!" Terry insisted.

Preschoolers are not known for their debating skills, so it went on like that for some time. But ultimately we figured out a way to *prove* it one way or another.

As we'd both learned from watching the *Super Friends* cartoon on television, Superman had super-hearing. We'd also learned from *Super Friends* that Superman was inclined to visit children on the smallest of pretexts. He might fly in with a *whoosh* to encourage them to brush their teeth, for instance.

Or he might teach them how to fold a paper airplane. If we called for him, surely Superman would fly right to Terry's front yard in Taos, New Mexico—*if* he were real.

We were eating lunch, so after we finished our peanut-butter-and-jelly sandwiches, we tromped outside and started hollering for the Man of Steel as loudly as five-year-olds can.

He never showed up. And even though I had proven my point, I was a little disappointed. But my friend's faith was barely shaken.

"Well," Terry said with a shrug of his shoulders, "he's probably fighting someone in Metropolis."

OF FAITH AND FABLE

We've already looked at how the stories we consume are powerful—be they in books or movies, television or video games. We've learned, biologically, how elements within these stories, and the technology used to communicate them, can affect us in significant ways.

But what about the stories themselves?

I'm not talking about whether a story is wildly violent or alarmingly sensual or startlingly profane. In many ways that stuff is mere window dressing to the story itself. Yes, of course it's important to be mindful of inappropriate content. But there are larger issues at work here. *How* a story is told isn't as important as *what* is being told, and why. What is the story telling us about how our world works? How people behave? About the ways we find meaning in our lives?

That, inherently, comes down to what our storytellers—and what we story consumers—*believe.*

Because of *Super Friends*, my own friend believed that Superman was real. And honestly, I wanted to believe that too. While you could say that a five-year-old might be prone to believe just about anything, let's be honest: The stories we absorb as teens and adults can impact us mightily too. They can shape how we think, how we feel, and how we believe.

While my *Plugged In* colleagues and I count swear words and detail inappropriate content in the movies we review, the most significant thing we watch for in movies, television shows, and other entertainment that comes across our screens is what a story is teaching you and your children to believe. A scene of horrific bloodiness can give your kids nightmares. A scene of inappropriate sexual behavior can impact your kids in loads of negative ways. But a story's worldview can shape your kids' worldviews. It can change how they live their lives, how they treat you and others, and how they interact (or don't interact) with God. It can mold how they work and how they play.

The worldview behind a story can even change the course of a country. After the 1915 release of the Civil War–era film *The Birth of a Nation*, the Ku Klux Klan went from a moribund movement to a dynamic, diabolical force in this nation's fabric.[1] In the wake of Disney's *Bambi*, hunting numbers dropped by 50 percent.[2] The 1993 movie *Philadelphia*—about a gay lawyer who contracts AIDS and is quickly fired from his firm—was credited with not just destigmatizing the disease but also introducing many Americans to perhaps the first homosexual they'd ever met, albeit in the guise of Tom Hanks, a straight actor portraying a homosexual character.

(Iconic film reviewer Roger Ebert called it "a righteous first step.")[3]

Don't think the movies, music, and television shows we consume today are any less influential. When it comes to what we believe, entertainment plays an important role in shaping those beliefs in us and our children. A joke in the 2022 gay rom-com *Bros* drove this point home. A gay man named Bobby (Billy Eichner) is told that half the kids in someone's kindergarten class identify as nonbinary. Bobby's not surprised. "We had AIDS," he says. "They had *Glee*."[4]

SPINNING A NEW WEB

In the 2019 movie *Spider-Man: Far from Home*,[5] Spidey must deal with a guy named Quentin Beck. But instead of being a typical supervillain who makes no secret of his evil intent, Beck masquerades as a superhero—the great, sacrificial Mysterio. Beck fools people through *story*, utilizing heroic tropes and soaring language and some really impressive special effects. Through this storytelling sleight of hand, he convinces Spider-Man and a host of others that he's the *good* guy, coming from a far-off dimension to save our world from powerful monsters known as the Elementals. When Spidey finally wises up, the master storyteller Mysterio twists the narrative, framing our friendly neighborhood Spider-Man as its villain.

Looking at just his raw power, Mysterio is a bit *meh* by Marvel supervillain standards. He has no superstrength or ability to manipulate minds. But as a storyteller, Mysterio rocks the foundations of this superhero saga, and others to come. His storytelling magic is so powerful, it sets in motion the events of the sequel, *Spider-Man: No Way Home*, wherein the fabric of space and time is sundered. Even when Mysterio is defeated, his lies live on. Such is the strength of a compelling story.

Why were Mysterio's fabrications so powerful, so influential? Because he understood the potency of *belief*. And he used that understanding for his own twisted ends. "People need to believe," he said in *Spider-Man: Far from Home*. "And nowadays, they'll believe anything."[6]

Belief. The word packs a wallop because it's central to who we are and why we're here. What we believe and who we believe in essentially form the path for how we live our lives. That path tells us where we are and where we're going. What we believe—not just what we *say* we believe, but what we truly do—shapes our thoughts, our decisions, and our relationships. The substance of our belief is more important to who we are than our arms or legs. And deep down, we all believe in *something*. In fact, we need to. It's how we're built.

As Christians, when we hear the word *belief*, we automatically think about our belief in God. Belief is interwoven with and indivisible from our faith. Pastor and author A. W. Tozer famously wrote, "What comes into our minds when we think about God is the most important thing about us."[7] The great apologist C. S. Lewis countered, "How we think of Him is of no importance except in so far as it is related to how He thinks of us."[8] Both are right, in part because you can't separate one from the other. Our concept of and belief in God are wrapped up in *relationship*, a love both given and received.

That relationship has often been manifested in the stories we tell and the songs we sing. Those narratives—those bits of *entertainment*, if you will—bolster our faith and serve as a thread linking believers through generations. The Psalms sing God's praises and weep over the suffering we endure. We hear their echoes in the spirituals sung in antebellum cotton fields, in the folk music of the fifties, in the worship music belted out in congregations around the world today.

But *belief* is not a strictly Christian, or even strictly religious, term. In the post-Christian world we live in, where belief in God dips with each passing year, and where church attendance is now below 50 percent,[9] our society's need for belief is increasingly untethered.

We need to believe in something. As such, some of us are more susceptible to believing anything. We see that in pop culture's screen-based stories.

GODS OF ALL KINDS

Ours is an age of patchwork belief systems. Lots of people today are still nominally Christian. Many more believe in *some* sort of God. But more and more people are willing to make God in their own image—and the younger they are, the more likely that'll happen. A 2017 study by the Pew Research Center found that more than a quarter of Americans labeled themselves "spiritual, not religious."[10] Another Pew survey, this one from 2019, found that 45 percent of American teens believe that "many religions can be true."[11]

When it comes to individual issues, the studies are even more striking. A 2014 Pew survey found that more than half of American Christians felt that society should accept homosexuality. Pew says that "this trend is driven partly by younger church members, who are generally more accepting of homosexuality than their elder counterparts." Even within the conservative confines of evangelical Protestantism that holds true: Slightly more than half (51 percent) of evangelical millennials believe homosexuality should be accepted, while just a third of evangelical Baby Boomers felt the same.[12]

While secular entertainment rarely talks about religion seriously, we do see that society is more and more willing to present us with multiple gods even if it is not inclined to proselytize for multiple religions.

The works of writer Neil Gaiman are particularly interesting in this vein. While atheists are quick to claim Gaiman as one of their own, his personal sense of spirituality is rather elusive. But it's clear that he is comfortable spelunking in the caves of the divine. In most of his best-known works—be it *American Gods* (which became a series on Starz) or *Good Omens* (a television series he created for Amazon Prime Video, based on a book he cowrote with Terry Pratchett) or *The Sandman* (a comic series he made for DC Comics that found its way to Netflix)—Gaiman features all manner of gods and goddesses, demigods, and demons. *The Sandman* movie features godlike characters pulled straight from Gaiman's imagination. But he liberally plucks from plenty of real-world pantheons as well. *American Gods* gives us an interesting showdown between the "old gods" (the Norse deity Odin, the Egyptian god Thoth, the Hindu god Ganesha, etc.) and new ones that we often worship ourselves: Technical Boy, Media, Mr. World, and so on. *Good Omens* culls more explicitly from Christianity, positing an unlikely partnership between an angel and a demon to prevent Armageddon.

The gods and demigods in Gaiman's work, even those that have Judeo-Christian underpinnings, are like those of ancient mythologies. The supernatural beings here are powerful, yes. They have influence over the lives of us mortals, no question. But they're also filled with their own selfishness, their own ambitions, their own jealousies, their own rivalries. Rather than being witness to the Fall, they themselves are a product of it.

It's telling that Gaiman cut his creative teeth in the world of comic books and studied at the knee of Alan Moore, the creator of the wildly influential DC Comics book series *Watchmen*.[13] That series likewise pondered the influence of godlike beings and how they'd interact with humanity. Dr. Manhattan—blessed with Superman-like abilities— loses interest in truth, justice, and the American way. Instead, he leaves for a galaxy "less complicated."

But the world of comic books (and the movies that followed them) has long played in the heavens—plucking characters who, if not gods themselves, have godlike powers. The cinematic arc of one of those characters—Thor, god of thunder—is particularly illustrative.

In the movie *Thor*, the creators take pains to tell us that neither Thor nor any of his compatriots are actually deities. "We are not gods," Odin tells his son, Loki. "We're born, we live, we die, just as humans do."

"Give or take five thousand years," Loki adds.[14]

And in *The Avengers*, Natasha Romanoff (Black Widow) and Captain America have this famous exchange:

"These guys come from legend," Black Widow says. "They're basically gods."

"There's only one God, ma'am," Cap says, "and I'm pretty sure He doesn't dress like that."[15]

As time has gone on, Marvel movies have more firmly ensconced Thor as a galactic deity, just one of many in a cosmos filled with gods and goddesses. In *Thor: Love and Thunder*, we see literally thousands of them—from the classical Greek god Zeus to a deified dumpling—and most of them are kind of jerks. No wonder that the movie's main antagonist, Gorr, seeks to kill them all.

Above these gods lies another layer of godlike beings. In *Love and Thunder*, we "meet" a faceless, emotionless entity called Eternity, who seems unwilling to interact with the galaxy unless someone asks it for a favor. In *Eternals*—perhaps Marvel's most explicitly "religious" movie to date, we meet the Celestials, incredibly powerful beings who seek to use humankind as sacrificial fuel for their own self-propagation.

The list goes on and on. *Moon Knight*'s story on Disney+ is filled with ancient Egyptian deities. In Loki's own Disney+ show, the self-proclaimed "god of mischief" discovers that his powers are no match for the bureaucracy of the Time Variance Authority (and the shadowy characters behind it).

None of these movies and shows are made with an eye toward actually rekindling faith in ancient or modern gods. Filmmakers aren't interested in moviegoers slapping up altars to sentient dumplings. But they do illustrate and, I think in their own way, encourage a cultural movement away from honest faith. All these imperfect, often immoral gods are not worthy of worship, so some young viewers *may* naturally wonder if our own God is likewise unworthy. And some stories—told frequently by agnostic or atheist storytellers— ask an underlying question: Should we, like Gorr, abandon faith and seek to kill the divine in our own lives?

What might faith be replaced with?

We all have to believe in *something*. We all have to believe that there is a grander purpose for our lives, or we believe there is not. We have to believe that there is objective moral good in play, or we believe there is not. We have to believe that our stories are part of a bigger story, or we believe they are not.

If we decide to reject the idea that belief in something greater than ourselves, something more just, more good, more merciful than we can be, we inevitably believe in a cold, random, unfeeling, uncaring cosmos. And if that is what we believe, how can we go on? How can we find meaning in a universe without it?

The movies have many answers, but three branches seem to predominate.

Me-ism

Back in ancient Greece, an entire school of philosophy was founded on the idea that pleasure is really the highest goal we should have. It was dubbed *Epicureanism* (after, of course, its primary advocate, Epicurus). It was all about maximizing pleasure and minimizing pain, and it was quite influential back in the day. You can see why. Epicureans believed that this life is all we've got: No punishments or rewards are in the offing after we are, well, offed. A full life is a rich life loaded with plenty of intellectual, emotional, and sensate pleasures.

We see plenty of modern-day Epicureans on our screens, of course—often as a prelude to a Hollywood finger wag that, hey, there is more to life than just sex, booze, and pleasure. But in one of the ironies that Hollywood seems to excel at, such movies saturate us in all that selfish hedonism before telling us (rather unconvincingly at times) that this sort of selfish hedonism is a bad thing.

Take director Martin Scorsese's *The Wolf of Wall Street*, which details (and exaggerates) the real-life career of stockbroker Jordan Belfort (played by Leonardo DiCaprio), who founded the ludicrously corrupt brokerage firm Stratton Oakmont. Scorsese has claimed that the movie was intended as something of a cautionary tale emphasizing that we aren't *supposed* to revel in Belfort's Epicurean decadence. Just the opposite, in fact.

"The devil comes with a smile, you know?" Scorsese told the *Hollywood Reporter*.[16]

Okay, fine, but when you spend two hours and forty-five minutes of a three-hour movie showing Belfort's decadence—and just how much *fun* that decadence is—that message can get lost.

That's what we find in a lot of movies, especially R-rated comedies that revel in decadent revelry. Drugs are a laugh. Sex is a snort. Wake up hung over in another country? No harm done, right? At least the character lived through it. At least he lived it up.

We can certainly find plenty of cinematic examples of pure, unadulterated hedonism—what Paul pointed to in his first letter to the Corinthians when he said, "If the dead are not raised, 'Let us eat and drink, for tomorrow we die'" (1 Corinthians 15:32).

But often our movies take a more subtle, more subversive tack: They encourage us to live our lives for *ourselves*—even if others are hurt in the living. *La La Land*, an Oscar-winning musical romance from 2016, is a sweet, fun film that praises the ideal of self-realization.[17]

In the film, Mia is an aspiring actress, and Sebastian is an aspiring jazz musician. They strike up a romance, and for a while, everything goes rather smoothly, but soon their respective careers begin driving wedges between them. Their relationship ultimately fails, but their careers do not. Mia realizes her dream of becoming a famous movie star and, at the end of the movie, crosses paths with Sebastian one last time. They nod to each other—in recognition, in appreciation, and perhaps even with a wistful sense of what might've been. But you know that Mia wouldn't trade her success, or her gift, for something as base as a relationship. The apostle Paul might've said that "the greatest of these is love" (1 Corinthians 13:13), but Mia knows better. The greatest end of all is seeing your name on a movie marquee.

La La Land is hardly an outlier. Movies frequently have characters who give up their families for careers, their spouses for their true loves, their responsibilities for happiness. Never mind that this kind of happiness is often fleeting, that true love of this sort rarely lasts, that careers ultimately end.

Nihilism

Rarely do movies tell us that the world is an awful place, that we should just sit in our closets and wait for the inevitable, painful end. But when society kills the things it has always believed in—the values it holds and the virtues it embraces, all of which stem from our creator—where do we go? Hedonism and "me-ism" may dull the pain for a time. But ultimately, those without God and the purpose He gives us must face the only logical alternative: an existence without meaning. A reality where we are simply accidents of evolution—what my pastor has been known to call "lucky mud."

Where does that leave us? In the Coen Brothers' Oscar-winning movie *No Country for Old Men*, we see where. The name of the movie hints at the void left behind by abandoned values. Two old men—Sheriff Bell (played by Tommy Lee Jones) and a colleague gripe about the degradation of society. They talk about how "the money and the drugs" have corrupted culture—a nod to growing hedonism. "Signs and wonders," Sheriff Bell sighs, referencing the Bible. "But I think once you quit hearing 'sir' and 'ma'am,' the rest is soon to follow."[18]

Then they begin to talk about the mysterious killer in their midst—the dead-end embodiment of where that lack of values ultimately leads. Anton Chigurh (Javier Bardem) kills without hesitation and without mercy. And he often kills, tellingly, with a gun attached to an air compressor—the same weapon used to kill cattle in slaughterhouses. The message is clear: We are, simply, meat to him—nothing sacred, nothing special. We are meat. And often he kills based on the flip of a coin—again, pointing to Chigurh's idea that the universe is a cold, empty, and ultimately random place.

In 2008—the year after *No Country for Old Men* was released—came another film carrying a tote full of nihilism. It was called *The Dark Knight*,[19] and it even featured a bad guy who based his deeds on the flip of a coin. Harvey Dent (Aaron Eckhart) started out as a good guy. But after being horrifically disfigured on one side of his body, he loses his belief and turns into Two-Face.

"You thought we could be decent men in an indecent time," he says to Batman (pointing out, as Sheriff Bell did, society's dwindling values). "But you were wrong. The world is cruel. And the only morality in a cruel world is chance. Unbiased. Unprejudiced. Fair."

But as bleak as Two-Face's philosophy might be, it pales in comparison to the movie's ultimate villain. In the opening sequence, Batman's archenemy, the Joker, is busy robbing a bank—and killing all his henchmen while he's at it. The bank's manager, tied up in the lobby, is horrified by what he sees the Joker doing. He's not scared as much as *offended*: The man (who seems to have some ties to the underworld himself) is horrified not by the robbery but by the lack of loyalty and decorum the Joker shows.

"Criminals in this town used to *believe* in things," the man says. "Honor. Respect. Look at you! What do *you* believe in, huh? What do *you* believe?"

"I believe [that] whatever doesn't kill you simply makes you . . . *stranger*," the Joker says. And he stuffs a smoke grenade into the man's mouth, then drives away. He's a nihilist, straight and simple, with a desire to (as Batman's loyal butler, Alfred, tells us) "watch the world burn."

"[Humanity's] morals, their code—it's a bad joke," the Joker says to Batman. "Dropped at the first sign of trouble. They're only as good as the world allows them to be. I'll show you. When the chips are down, these . . . civilized people? They'll eat each other.

"I'm not a monster," he adds. "I'm just ahead of the curve."

So in a world without God, what can bring meaning to a meaningless world? Many movies tell us that *we* can.

Humanism

Released in 1993, *Groundhog Day*,[20] starring Bill Murray, earned reasonably favorable reviews and respectable business at the box office. But in the years since, the film, directed by Harold Ramis, has become one of American cinema's all-time classics. And much of that is because of its deeply philosophical and even spiritual themes.

In the film, cynical weatherman Phil Connors (Murray) travels to Punxsutawney, Pennsylvania, with his producer, Rita (Andie MacDowell), and cameraman, Larry (Chris Elliott), to cover the local groundhog's annual emergence from his burrow to see (or not see) his shadow. But somehow, Phil gets locked in a forever-looping day, where every day is February 2. And he can't escape from it.

Interestingly, he follows all the worldviews we've already outlined.

When Phil realizes what's going on—he's stuck in a cycle of apparently meaningless days—he at first dives into hedonistic "me-ism." He overeats. He sleeps around. He steals money. Why? Because he knows he'll never have to pay the consequences for anything he does. Even if he lands in prison (which he does), he'll be back in his bed at the bed-and-breakfast the following morning. Or, rather, *this* morning.

But all that excess ultimately proves to be unfulfilling. You can only eat so many pancakes and sleep with so many women before you long for something more meaningful. Despite living this Epicurean dream, Phil sinks into a nihilist state of mind. This endless cycle of days feels utterly meaningless. He'd like nothing better than to watch the world burn—as long as he can burn with it. He commits suicide in a variety of ways, hoping, finally, to find freedom the only way he feels is possible: through death. Ashes to ashes, dust to dust, Groundhog Day to ground.

But each attempt is unsuccessful, so that's clearly not the answer either.

And then, one Groundhog Day, he confesses his plight to Rita, who encourages him not to think of this endless cycle as a curse but as a *blessing*. After that conversation, Phil walks into the next Groundhog Day in a much different state of mind: He will live to improve the lives of those around him.

Groundhog Day has been used to illustrate central tenants of many religions, including Christianity. Phil's turn toward selflessness reflects how Jesus wants us to deal with the world around us, too: Love others as we would be loved. That's a totally valid way of looking at the film.

But *Groundhog Day* is also, underneath its metaphysical trappings, a deeply humanistic tale. We don't see Phil pray to God or bow toward Mecca or engage in Buddhist meditations. While there certainly seems to be a cosmic consciousness that wants to teach Phil *something*, he doesn't see or acknowledge who that being might be. His endless days float by without the anchor of faith. When he turns his attention to helping others, he has no assurance that he'll ever break out of the cycle. In fact, he stops even trying. The meaning he finds is not in hedonism or nihilism, but it's not in religion either. Rather, Phil discovers that the only path to meaning is through bettering himself. No rescue is coming *for* him. God, if there is a God, seems to have forgotten him. Whatever salvation is in the offing rests entirely on his shoulders.

Narratively, there's a fine line between this sort of humanism and a more spiritual epiphany. In fact, you could argue that most movies are humanistic in this sense. Few cinematic heroes look for salvation through prayer. If they're going to save their girlfriend or boyfriend, the city or the world, they'll have to do it *themselves*, by golly. Most of these stories don't contradict Christian faith. Indeed, they can often walk parallel with it.

But the movies don't draw the line for you. A Christian can see Phil's growth as a sign that he's on the right path, and that path ultimately leads to Jesus. But a humanist can look at the same growth and not see God in it at all. A humanist believes that we can and should help people because it's the right thing to do. Why is it right? Because we humans say it's the right thing to do. We make up our own definitions of what right and wrong are.

But, of course, this means that, for the humanist, right and wrong can vary widely. And good and evil can change with the times.

Which brings us to where we are now: a deeply moral age in which morality is not eternal—given by an all-knowing, all-loving God—but a moving target. Because secular morality's human makers are always moving too. Sometimes today's humanistic morality walks right alongside the inculcated, time-honored truths of the Bible. For example, the Golden Rule—treating people with love and respect—is still very much in vogue (or, at least, people like the theory). At other times, society's values and biblical values clash. (LGBT issues are, of course, a prime example of that.) At still other moments, culture unveils "new" values that even Christians themselves might weigh differently. Environmentalism can feel, to some, deeply biblical, what with our call to be stewards of the earth (and the clearly loving natural imagery the Bible often gives us). But others believe that environmentalism threatens to become a pagan religion unto itself.

The beliefs and values we see in our entertainment can demand some thought and (as we'll see in a later chapter) a good grounding in our Christian beliefs and values. If we don't really know what *we* believe—or if our children don't— that can leave us open to plenty of influence from the movies we watch.

But there's another factor in play. Belief—especially in the world of story—can sometimes be a two-way street. It's not just about what the movie or its makers believe. It's what you believe too.

BELIEF, BACK AT YOU

I'm a big Batman fan, so let's zip back to *The Dark Knight* and revisit the Joker and his nihilist philosophy.

In the closing minutes of the movie, the Joker conducts a social experiment, just to prove that his brand of nihilism is, indeed, ahead of the curve. He wires two ships filled with explosives. One ship is filled with some of Gotham's worst criminals, and the other with everyday Joes and Janes. Each ship also comes with a trigger that can blow up the *other* one. The Joker tells the passengers on each ship that if someone on either vessel presses the button—killing hundreds of people—he'll let the survivors sail on their merry way. If someone doesn't, both ships are destined for destruction.

Funny thing, though: the passengers on both ships listen to the better angels of their nature. No one triggers the bombs, and Batman takes the opportunity to gloat (even as the Joker seems to have him trapped).

"What were you trying to prove?" Batman asks the Joker. "That deep down, everyone's as ugly as you? You're *alone*!"[21]

Now, I've seen the movie a few times, and I originally thought I was going to use this scene to illustrate humanism. Batman, I thought, had said something along the lines of "The city just showed you that it's filled with good people."

As Christians, we might suspect that that's not theologically true. As parents, we *know* it's not true. Leave a four-year-old to his own devices without correction, and you'll see a supervillain in the making—ready to lie and cheat and steal and hit if he can get away with it. People aren't *naturally* good; it's only through a work of the Holy Spirit, accompanied by our guidance, that our kids become "good." It's only through God that we even know what "good" is!

But, it turns out, that's not what Batman said at all.

"This city just showed you that it's full of people ready to *believe* in good," Batman tells the Joker. That little twist makes a massive difference.

What does it mean to "believe in good"?

A humanist might have one answer. A hedonist might have another. A nihilist might smirk and say, "Good? No such thing."

But for Christians, we know what it means to believe in good. It means to believe in God. It means to believe in the sort of morality that doesn't change with the times and goes well beyond what we *feel* like doing at any given moment. The good we see—the good seen in the people on those ships—is that life is sacred. That life is worth preserving. That sacrificing ourselves for others is a noble thing indeed. And when we look at Batman—a guy who's trying to do the right thing in a corrupt and often unappreciative culture, a guy who sees the flaws in the world but also chooses to believe that it can be made better—we can see, potentially, a hero who looks at the world a little like we do.

The Dark Knight isn't a Christian movie by any stretch. It, like *Groundhog Day* and *Thor: Love and Thunder* and literally thousands of other movies out there, can be used to illustrate plenty of different values and beliefs. The same work can be seen and interpreted in different ways. It's not just about what the storyteller believes; it's about what the viewer or listener or reader believes too. We can draw lessons from unexpected quarters. We can show our children that certain characters can teach us things—even when those characters are flawed or fail.

Yes, it's important to understand how the culture's storytellers are trying to influence us. But we don't have to let that wash over us with the passivity of pebbles at the bottom of a riverbed. We can be like trees, drinking in what is worthwhile. We can be like dams, pushing back against that which is not. More than that, we are the people of Christ, equipped with the most important truths, the most beautiful beliefs, in the universe.

When I was hollering for Superman as a little boy, he never came. But Jesus *did* come. And He, and everything He stands for, is with us still—in the movies, in our living rooms, in our libraries and dance halls. We bring our beliefs along wherever we go. Those beliefs shape what we think and feel about every other belief system—every other "-ism"—we face.

And that is, as Gandalf once said to a young hobbit wrestling with right and wrong in a far different world, "an encouraging thought."[22]

DARK NIGHT

Actor Heath Ledger died in February 2008—nearly six months before *The Dark Knight* was released. Still, he went on to win an Oscar for his portrayal of the Joker in Christopher Nolan's groundbreaking superhero movie. More than a decade later, Joaquin Phoenix won his own Academy Award for portraying the clown. While Phoenix's Joker feels much different from Ledger's—as much a victim of an evil society as an evil himself—both seem to share a core belief: It's a broken world. Let's break it back.

The Joker is one of culture's most influential storytellers. Yes, he's supposed to be the villain, but he's a charismatic and convincing one. The character plays on some of our darkest fears and, perhaps our even darker hopes. His image could, and can, be seen everywhere, from T-shirts to coffee cups.

And while most viewers understand that his belief structure leads to oblivion and root for his defeat, some embrace Gotham's greatest villain and his message. Writes Andrew Bloom of Ledger's Joker in the online publication *Consequence*, "That id-fueled mentality, which bucks any attempt to impose order, found particular purchase in a growing number of young men who found themselves coming of age in a society that they felt had no place for them."[23]

In the 2012 Aurora, Colorado, movie-theater shooting, a man opened fire on a theater packed with people watching *The Dark Knight Rises*. Moviegoers speculated, as have many others, that the killer was inspired by Ledger's Joker. And when Phoenix's *Joker* movie was released in 2019, a number of survivors of the Aurora shooting worried that this film might trigger more violence.

"I don't need to see a picture of [the Aurora shooter]," Sandy Phillips, whose daughter was one of the twelve people killed in the shooting, told the *Hollywood Reporter*. "I just need to see a *Joker* promo and I see a picture of the killer."[24]

PART 2

What You Can Do

Christ on Your Couch

Kennedy Unthank

IN THE PREVIOUS CHAPTER, we saw that belief is a surprisingly big part of our relationship with entertainment. Everyone believes in *something*—even if they believe that there is no greater force to believe in. Intentionally or not, those who tell our culture's most powerful stories bring their beliefs into the entertainment they create.

Of course, as consumers of media and entertainment, we bring our beliefs into the mix as well.

But *how* exactly do we bring our beliefs—our faith—into the world of entertainment? How do we look at movies and television shows, social media and technology, through the prisms of our own understanding of God, and of meaning, and of life itself?

Let's explore that a bit.

FAITH SHAPES OUR LIVES

Once upon a time, long before I arrived on the scene, my father was attending Texas Tech University. It was about a week before the first semester began, and because he was a resident assistant in the dorm, he was already on campus with the rest of the RAs.

That week, a few of the other RAs asked my father if he'd like to watch a movie or two with them, and he accepted. As they rode the elevator up to the viewing room, he found out that one of the movies was a 1992 neo-noir erotic thriller called *Basic Instinct*, which became infamous for a certain interrogation scene (among many other sexual scenes).

My father told the group that because of the movie's extremely sensual content, he couldn't watch it with them, but he'd be interested in seeing the second film, which was much tamer.

"Which movie are you watching first?" he asked.

A female RA, who apparently found his response offensive, blurted out that they'd start the night with *Basic Instinct*. So my father replied that he couldn't stay but that they could invite him up to watch the second movie when the first one was finished. With that, he rode the elevator back downstairs. Needless to say, he wasn't invited back to watch the second movie, and the offended girl seemed to hold my father's rejection of *Basic Instinct* against him for months afterward.

Two years later, that same young woman approached my father and admitted that his comments had made her angry. For weeks she couldn't get them out of her head. But then she told my father that the encounter had made a huge impact on her. It was the main impetus for her questioning her own beliefs and choices, and she eventually became a Christian because of it.

Of course, my father couldn't have known what an impact his views would have on this woman. As far as he'd known, she still thought he was a jerk. But as a result of his decision to align his viewing habits with his Christian convictions, the Lord planted a seed in that woman's heart and eventually brought her to saving faith.

NOT ALL THINGS ARE HELPFUL

Why do I tell that story? Because it emphasizes an important biblical truth: Our faith as followers of Christ should influence *every aspect* of our lives. If it doesn't, we must ask ourselves how closely we're truly following Him.

Scripture repeatedly affirms this principle. The apostle James wrote that good works result from genuine faith and prove its existence (James 2:18). The apostle Paul wrote that we are called to do everything "for the glory of God" (1 Corinthians 10:31). Jesus Himself said that those who love Him will, with the help of the Holy Spirit, obey His teaching (John 14:23-26). What we believe should impact how we think, what we do, and how we treat others. If we keep our faith boxed up until Sunday-morning services or Wednesday-evening Bible studies, we're probably missing the point.

As Christians, we might choose not to engage in a certain activity for a multitude of reasons: It may be a clear sin or something that tempts us *toward* sin. It could prick our conscience, or we might not find it profitable or glorifying to God.

When we consider doing *all* things for the glory of God, that includes making entertainment choices. Some of us might find this a bit overbearing. Doesn't God's grace give Christians the liberty to watch whatever entertainment we want?

Consider Paul's response to this line of thinking: "'All things are lawful,' but not all things are helpful. 'All things are lawful,' but not all things build up" (1 Corinthians 10:23, ESV). That's true for us, and it's especially true for children. Certainly, much of what we find on our screens today does not help our sons or build up our daughters.

Paul's commission for us to do *all* things for the glory of God means that this mindset should encompass *every* aspect in our lives—including the entertainment choices we make for ourselves and our families. There are some things that entertain the world that Christians should abstain from— even if it's simply to set us apart from the world.

FAITH AND UNFAITHFUL ENTERTAINMENT

Discernment in entertainment choices isn't a new idea in the Christian community. Consider the writings of Athenagoras in the mid- to late second century. In *A Plea for the Christians*, he wrote the following:

Who does not reckon among the things of greatest interest the contests of gladiators and wild beasts, especially those which are given by you [the Romans]? But we [Christians], deeming that to

see a man put to death is much the same as killing
him, have abjured such spectacles.[1]

In context, Athenagoras's argument focuses on refuting a
popular claim in his day that Christians were cannibals and
murderers because they practiced Communion. Athenagoras
refuted the claim by stating that if Christians "abjured" the
Roman-sanctioned gladiatorial games so they would not
view the killing, how could they celebrate a Christian sacra-
ment that would involve killing?

Athenagoras's point reveals that the Christians of his day
felt that the gladiatorial games were an inappropriate form
of entertainment. Granted, one could argue that there's a big
difference between modern entertainment and the gladiatorial games—namely, that people actually died in the latter.
When we watch movies on the big screen, we don't need a
disclaimer stating that no actors were killed in the making of
our entertainment.

But there remains a question for the modern viewer: Even
if the on-screen violence and sex *are* fake, how far is too far
for us? We'll get to our kids in a moment. For now, let's
concentrate on our own choices as Christian adults. While
the answer is often up to the individual viewer, a couple of
biblical principles can help us discern whether screen content
goes too far.

First, Jesus calls us to "watch and pray so that you will not
fall into temptation" (Matthew 26:41), and Scripture commands us to flee from "youthful passions" (2 Timothy 2:22,
ESV). Proverbs 22:3 advises us to "take refuge" when we see

danger ahead. How might we apply these instructions to our entertainment choices?

Take, for example, two men who know they struggle with sexual sin. Both are invited to a party to watch the popular, sex-filled show *Game of Thrones*. One man, recognizing the inherent temptations that may arise from its sensual content, chooses not to watch the show and avoids being tempted. The other man, claiming he can handle the sensual content, watches the show, is tempted, and chooses to sin as a result. Both men were aware of their struggles with sexual sin, and both were aware of the sensual content in *Game of Thrones*. However, one of them brushed off the show as "no big deal" and opened himself up to temptation. Instead of fleeing from temptation, he attempted to justify engaging in it. In the words of Jesus, this man's eye caused him to sin, and he refused to "gouge it out and throw it away" (Matthew 5:29).

Not everyone who watches *Game of Thrones* will sin. But there's no question that the show—and others like it—is an avenue for temptation. In fact, HBO actually filed a lawsuit against the porn website Pornhub for showing sexually explicit clips from the show on its site.[2] According to Pornhub, traffic on its site dropped noticeably when a new *Game of Thrones* episode aired.

Often when we insist that our entertainment choices are "no big deal" or that they "don't affect me," we're lying to ourselves.

A second biblical principle to remember is that we are not to be stumbling blocks to the people around us. Writing to the Corinthians, Paul addressed a dispute among believers

CHRIST ON YOUR COUCH

over whether it was acceptable for Christians to eat food previously offered to idols (1 Corinthians 8). Though he confirmed that eating this food was appropriate for Christians, he added a caveat: "Be careful, however, that the exercise of your rights does not become a stumbling block to the weak" (verse 9). Our freedom to enjoy entertainment should not cause other believers to stumble in their faith. Just as I wouldn't serve alcohol to a friend who is a recovering alcoholic, I would also not queue up a movie that I know might cause someone to stumble—even if viewing the content itself isn't sinful.

A third biblical principle to keep in mind is that we need to exercise self-control in our entertainment choices. This principle is reflected in Galatians 5, where Paul identifies self-control as a fruit of the Spirit in a believer's life. Paul also reminds us that "the grace of God . . . teaches us to say 'No' to ungodliness and worldly passions, and to live self-controlled, upright and godly lives" (Titus 2:11-13). We need to remember that many of the seemingly harmless pleasures of this world that God allows us to enjoy can quickly become idols if we fail to practice self-control. In some instances, we can find ourselves spending too much time viewing screen-based entertainment, which can damage our relationships and, in extreme cases, degrade our physical and mental health.

In other instances, the entertainment we watch may pull us away from the timeless edicts of our faith. For instance, even casual viewers of modern entertainment have noticed a distinct spike in messaging that promotes LGBT relationships, which the Bible clearly tells us are sinful (Romans

1:26-27; 1 Corinthians 6:9-11). If we feel ourselves being swayed by worldly philosophies in our entertainment, we should exercise self-control and avoid these types of influences until we are better equipped spiritually to address them.

These three principles are by no means an exhaustive list, but as we apply them in our everyday lives, we'll start to appreciate how intertwined our faith is with the entertainment choices we make. That's a good thing for ourselves and our families, because if our Christian faith influences the entertainment we consume as parents, it will also influence the entertainment we allow our children to watch.

TRAINING UP OUR CHILDREN

As we discussed in chapter 3, the stories we ingest can have a big impact on us. Whether it's as simple as fostering a desire within us to share a story with others or as complex as reshaping the way we think, entertainment's alluring pull can cause even the wariest of us to become enthralled. That's especially true for children. After all, they don't start out their lives wary at all. They're inherently trusting. They tend to believe the messages they're given without regard to the source. And while children become more wary and even cynical with time (the average teenager is ample proof of that), that's no guarantee your children will be wary of the messages they should be wary of.

Therefore, it is essential that as parents we provide a solid biblical foundation for our children to stand on in the face of potentially harmful messages—especially in a world where entertainment is becoming more and more accessible. We should "train up" our children in a godly way, according to Proverbs 22:6 (ESV), but the media we allow in our homes isn't going to wait for us to do so before spreading its toxic messages. The entertainment will train up our children in its own subjective way.

When Do We Teach Them?

For parents, it can be easy to think that young children aren't ready to start thinking about the messages that media is teaching them. But we can turn to Scripture to provide us with the confidence to begin teaching and training our children at any age.

In Deuteronomy 6:5, we read about the time God gave Israel the most important commandment: "Love the LORD your God with all your heart and with all your soul and with all your strength." Directly afterward, God addressed parents: "These words that I command you today shall be on your heart. You shall teach them diligently to your children, and shall talk of them when you sit in your house, and when you walk by the way, and when you lie down, and when you rise" (verses 6-7, ESV).

Parents are specifically instructed to teach "these words"—to love God with all our hearts, souls, and strength—diligently to our children in every aspect of life. And lest we lie to ourselves by claiming that this command was only for the nation of Israel, the apostle Paul gives us a similar command: "Fathers, do not provoke your children to anger, but bring them up in the discipline and instruction of the Lord" (Ephesians 6:4, ESV).

It is never too early to begin teaching our children to follow God's ways. Of course, most parents already do this to some extent. We tell our kids that we shouldn't steal and that we should be nice to each other. These instructions are part of God's moral law, even if we don't specifically point that out. Each time we tell our kids that some behavior or belief is right or wrong, we impress on them a type of morality—either a morality based on subjective and arbitrary beliefs or a morality based on God's objective law. It is this latter morality to which Scripture refers when it commands us to "bring [our children] up in the discipline and instruction of the Lord."

In pursuit of this command, parents shouldn't wait for moral questions to come up. We need to be proactive—to start the work of answering questions before they're even asked. To build a strong moral foundation for our children, *we* should have the first say in what that morality should be. Not the school, not their friends, and *certainly* not the television. If we allow outside influences to be our children's first introduction to these moral issues, we'll be forced to spend much more time playing catch-up. If we don't teach our sons and daughters how to morally process sex and relationships, for example, our televisions will be more than happy to fill the gap.

How Do We Teach Them?

When we train our children, we must understand that some methods yield more fruit than others. Though it is ultimately up to each child to accept or reject training, the *way* we train our kids is another avenue for bringing them to Christ. Screaming a lesson at a child from across the room is less likely to work than personally guiding them through it. Remember that God doesn't want our parenting to provoke wrath in our children; if we're unkind or harsh, they'll be much less likely to accept our teaching— even if it *is* true!

How can parents gently yet firmly instruct our kids to follow the Lord? Though we should be teaching our children as early as possible, the depth of teaching should be age appropriate. Salvation issues—namely, faith in Christ's death and resurrection—should be taught unceasingly. General topics about God and His attributes (love, justice, anger toward evil, mercy, etc.) are also lessons that should be introduced early on.

For heavier topics—like LGBT issues, abortion, or premarital sex—you may want to wait until your children are a little older so they can better understand them. However, many parents consider it wise to introduce young children to these issues at an age-appropriate level to keep them from falling for the antibiblical messages they'll encounter. While it's up to each parent to discern when their child is ready for such talks, Focus on the Family recommends that heavier topics be approached during your child's preteen years to prepare them for the ideas they'll be exposed to in adolescence.

When you are discipling your children, remember that

some concepts and truths that seem simple to you now were at one point foreign and confusing. It will likely be the same way for your kids. Your knowledge of the Lord isn't a genetic trait that will automatically be passed on to your children, so your instruction will likely require you to answer questions that will force you to explain the *why* behind the *what*.

Parents should be well equipped to answer these *why* questions, because they'll naturally lead to a deeper understanding of the Christian faith. For instance, "Jesus died for our sins" explains *what* happened, but if our children know only this fact, they'll likely be unable to say *why* He died for our sins. But if we explain the reality of sin and how it separates us from God, and that Jesus died to take the punishment for our sins so that we can be seen as blameless before God, then our children will be better equipped to explain why it happened. In other words, the *what* sets the framework for belief, and the *why* gives justification for it.

Thankfully, the Lord has, in His mercy and wisdom, made *Why?* the favorite question of all young children! Most parents are already used to answering it.

What happens when the secular world introduces unbiblical ideas to your children before you have a chance to address them? In this case, you'll likely need to do some backtracking with your kids to pave the way for proper instruction. Since the world has already introduced a *what* to your children, it's up to you to explain *why* that *what* is incorrect. This correction will lead to exposing the flaws in this worldly thinking while revealing why the biblical standard is best. If your children bring up arguments in favor of unbiblical ideas—whether they have been directly taught to believe these ideas or have been persuaded when encountering them online—try to avoid reacting with anger. You don't want to discourage your children from asking more questions or exploring issues further with you. Doing so may root the false ideas even deeper in their hearts and minds. Instead, try to show your children *why* such arguments fail so they can reject them of their own volition rather than simply trying to please you or avoid (or end) an argument.

All this may (understandably) feel a bit overwhelming. So let me set your mind at ease. No parent—no matter how good or well-meaning or God-fearing they might be—will successfully lay the moral groundwork for *every* issue before a child starts absorbing lessons from the culture. Even if such a parent existed, their children would always be asking *why* and might continue questioning their parents' lessons throughout their lives. In fact, most young people, at some point, hear persuasive arguments on the other side of a debate that they'll want to test against the truth you've given them. (And they'll probably want to test *you* at times as well!) Parenting is more art than science, and it's a messy art at that. With these concessions in mind, we encourage parents, above all else, to *pray*. The Lord grants wisdom to those who ask for it (James 1:5) and provides instruction and comfort (Romans 15:4).

AN IMPORTANT TRUTH

Though it is our duty as Christian parents to instruct our children in the ways of the Lord, we have no duty, power, or authority to *save* them. The truth is that no one comes to Jesus unless the Father draws them to Himself (John 6:44). However, we should always seek to live and speak in a way that reflects the glory of God and guides our children toward salvation.

Even if you were the best possible Christian parent—teaching your children all the ways of the Lord—your children still might not come to faith (or heed your advice in other areas either). Nothing you say or do guarantees that your children will accept Christ as their Lord and Savior. If you have done your best to teach them about the Lord and they don't come to faith in Christ, it isn't because you didn't say or do enough.

TRAINED FOR THE TV

As mentioned earlier, entertainment often comes with subtle and not-so-subtle messages, and if we're not careful, we just might unintentionally consume those messages with as much ease as we do a favorite snack. Even if we neglect to recognize the powerful influence entertainment can have on us, the secular world is embracing it. Take, for instance, actress Olivia Rodrigo's *Hollywood Life* interview, in which she discussed the influence *High School Musical: The Musical: The Series* had in casting her character with two lesbian mothers:

> My character has two moms, and I loved the way that they did that. They just portrayed it as completely normal and natural, which . . . that's just real life. And it's not a statement, it's not a punchline; it's just how it is. . . . TV [can] transform how you see the world. . . . It's a really important thing, *especially for younger viewers to see.* I'm really excited for that.[3]

Did you catch that? Rodrigo believes that it's especially important for younger viewers to watch shows that portray lesbian mothers. As long as parents are willing to let their children consume secular entertainment created by secular people, these issues will come up. We cannot be caught off guard. So when unbiblical agendas inevitably arise in your child's entertainment, how can you handle them?

DO NOT BE CONFORMED

As Christians consuming secular entertainment, it's helpful to remind ourselves of the apostle Paul's words to the church in Rome: "Do not be conformed to this world, but be transformed by the renewal of your mind, that by testing you may discern what is the will of God, what is good and acceptable and perfect" (Romans 12:2, esv).

It's interesting that Paul talked about *testing* to determine what the will of God is. What does that testing process look like? How does it happen?

We're told that the renewal of our minds—the knowledge and belief in God's Word brought through salvation—helps us discern what is and isn't good according to God's holy standard. Paul explained this concept of renewal more fully in his letter to the church in Ephesus:

> You were dead in the trespasses and sins in which
> you once walked, following the course of this world,
> following the prince of the power of the air, the spirit
> that is now at work in the sons of disobedience—
> among whom we all once lived in the passions of
> our flesh, carrying out the desires of the body and
> the mind, and were by nature children of wrath, like
> the rest of mankind. But God, being rich in mercy,
> because of the great love with which he loved us,
> even when we were dead in our trespasses, made us
> alive together with Christ—by grace you have been
> saved—and raised us up with him and seated us with
> him in the heavenly places in Christ Jesus, so that in

the coming ages he might show the immeasurable
riches of his grace in kindness toward us in Christ
Jesus. For by grace you have been saved through
faith. And this is not your own doing; it is the gift of
God, not a result of works, so that no one may boast.
For we are his workmanship, created in Christ Jesus
for good works, which God prepared beforehand,
that we should walk in them.

EPHESIANS 2:1-10, ESV

As Christians, all of us once walked with the rest of the world "in the passions of our flesh." We were "children of wrath" and death, like the rest of the world. But then God, through His grace, "made us alive together with Christ" and revealed His truth to us. It is our knowledge of God through His Word that helps us combat the false ideas that threaten to conform us to the world.

When such ideas appear on our television screens before the eyes of our impressionable children, we can't ignore them. We must be prepared to talk about them. If necessary, we should pause the show and talk through the issues with our children, helping them see the errors in the ideas presented.

We must also help our children learn how to guard their hearts and discern the good from the bad. Just as we were once in need of (and sometimes *still* need) guidance through complex issues, so do our children. Ask your children what they think about the messages they receive from entertainment, and make a point to ask whether they agree—and why.

Then discuss with them whether those messages are right or wrong and guide them toward an answer that accords with God's truth.

We need to remind our children that God's love for humanity necessarily implies that He would want to keep us safe from harm—even if we don't understand how harmful something might be. Just as a child might not learn the danger of a hot stove until they touch it, we often don't understand God's warnings against certain things until we get hurt too. People will tell us that some things are okay to do even when God says that they *aren't* okay. Although we may not understand why God is telling us that something is wrong, we can look back on how He has remained faithful in other aspects of our lives and trust that He is surely faithful in this part of it too.

Most importantly, while the television is paused and you're discussing these things with your children, use this teaching moment to point back to the truth of the gospel: that God the Father sent His Son, Jesus Christ, to earth to save us from our sins, including the sins in our entertainment. He did this by living a perfect life in accordance with God's moral law and willfully dying on the cross in our place, taking our sins and the subsequent wrath of God upon Himself and providing for us His blameless righteousness. Then He rose from the dead, proving that He is Lord and that His promise of salvation is forever for all who repent and believe in this message.

This salvation renews our minds and helps us guard our hearts so we can discern what is "good and acceptable and perfect" not only in our entertainment but in all other aspects of life as well (Romans 12:2).

———

The message communicated in this chapter may not be pleasant to hear. You may even feel that such a strong case has been made against entertainment that you're ready to swear it off altogether. But fleeing from entertainment because there's a risk of ungodly or dangerous content is not the point. My *Plugged In* colleagues and I have no qualms about enjoying entertainment; rather, we want to help families guard against the harmful messages it promotes. In fact, we would encourage enjoying a video game or movie with your family as a way to bond with them.

Movies, TV shows, and video games can be a great way for families to connect. I distinctly recall playing countless games of *Mario Kart: Double Dash!!* with my father and brothers while growing up, and I would sit down to watch the new *MythBusters* episode with my dad every Wednesday. I will cherish these memories for as long as I live. Movies also led naturally into amazing conversations about faith with my dad—such as about Gandalf's fight with the Balrog, his death, and his shining return from the dead in *The Lord of the Rings* trilogy as a symbolic representation of Jesus Christ crushing the head of the serpent.

Try to think of entertainment as malleable. Yes, some entertainment is objectively bad, and consuming it can lead to some nasty habits. But it's good to think of entertainment in general as a malleable thing. It can be used for good purposes and bad purposes. Consider the way Paul addresses food in 1 Corinthians 8: "Food will not commend us to God. We are no worse off if we do not eat, and no better off if we do. But take care that this right of yours does not somehow becoming a stumbling block to the weak" (verses 8-9, ESV). In the same way, consuming entertainment depends on you, on the context, and on the entertainment itself.

Your faith has an impact on your children, so as you consider entertainment choices as a family, help them learn what it means to bring glory to the Lord in all things—even in such simple choices. Help them learn how to guard their hearts, and teach them how to enjoy their favorite shows without being swept away in the persuasive messaging. Ask the Lord for guidance and discernment as a family so that the passions of this world won't be able to compete or compare in any way with the shining glory of God's truth.

Who knows? Perhaps, like my father on that campus years ago, as you live out your convictions, God just might plant a seed in someone's heart and call that person to faith in Him.

The Game Plan

Adam R. Holz

WHEN I SAY THE WORD *REVOLUTION*, what do you think of?

Depending on your age and schooling, maybe you immediately think about *history*: the American Revolution, the French Revolution, or the Russian Revolution (three very different historical moments with far-reaching implications).

Or maybe you think about *technology*: the advent of the printing press, the internal combustion engine, electricity, the internet (the latter of which I'll talk about more in a moment).

Or maybe you think about *seasons of vast cultural change* that impact the very ways we think about life and what it means to be human: periods like the Enlightenment or the countercultural pushback that reshaped American society and public mores in the 1960s.

Here's the thing about revolutions though: Typically, we only understand them looking *backward*, with the benefit of hindsight. Only the passage of time gives us the perspective to see clearly just how much a given revolution changed the way we understand life, the shape of everyday living, and our expectations about what our day-to-day existence should ideally look like.

Now, you might be wondering why I'm talking about revolutions in a book about helping your family navigate the intertwined worlds of entertainment and technology. Here's why: Whether you realize it clearly or not, we're in the midst of a revolution that arguably might be the most significant in human history. It's been called the *information revolution*. The advent of the internet in the mid-1990s paired with technology that enables us to access its vast troves of content from anywhere at any time is a revolution on par with any major technological or cultural shift in history. And we're all living through it.

THE REVOLUTION WILL BE DIGITIZED

Those born since the turn of the millennium have been called *digital natives*. Access to information and entertainment anywhere, at any time, is just part of their existence. It's the water in which they swim.

But for those of us who are, to varying degrees, older, we have seen the landscape of entertainment change dramatically in the course of our lifetimes.

I was born in 1970. During my formative years, I watched television—the kind with a manual rotary channel dial and a lovely twelve-inch black-and-white screen. The TV had a whopping four channels: the three broadcast networks plus PBS. I also listened to music on vinyl records, which by the late 1970s began to give way to more portable formats.

Speaking of the 1970s, my father was an early adopter of new technology in those days. I fondly remember when he came home with our first VCR in 1979. Want to guess what he paid? A mind-boggling three thousand dollars! Can you imagine? I recall with equal fondness the day when I first went to a video store to rent a movie. I walked in, saw all those VHS (and competing Sony Betamax) cases on the walls, and felt as though my eyes had been opened to the knowledge of good and evil. (Well, not really, but it was a transformative moment.) No longer were movies like summer vacation—there for a few weeks and then gone, never to be seen again. There, on the shelves, were films that were years—no, *decades*—old. It blew my mind that we could pick whatever we wanted, take it home with us, and then watch it whenever we wanted.

That moment in 1979 foreshadowed an entertainment and technology revolution that would gather momentum in the eighties and nineties. Cable TV went from being a novelty in the mid-seventies to widespread usage by the end of the eighties. Now, instead of four channels, we had fifty or sixty. The digital revolution was fully underway as well, with cassette tapes soon giving way to compact discs. (*I don't have to rewind or fast-forward? I don't have to worry about the tape wearing out and breaking?*) Video games were relatively common as well. And a few lucky families were rumored to have something called a *computer.*

In the nineties, the nascent World Wide Web, which was first used largely by government researchers to share information, was on the brink of changing everything. Websites soon went from fun little "add-ons" for newspapers and magazines to replacing them completely.

I got my first cell phone in 1997. Just two years before, I'd flown by myself to Asia—without a phone. Can you imagine traveling overseas without a phone?

Once the calendar rolled into 2000 and Y2K didn't destroy everything (I think I still have some propane if you need it), the changes in the way we accessed and consumed information accelerated. Apple's iPod helped pave the way for the iPhone. Meanwhile, Amazon, Google, Facebook, and YouTube were busy upending the ways we interacted with commerce and communicated with friends. These companies would soon be joined by the likes of Instagram, Spotify, and myriad others in an ever-accelerating stream of constant digital connection.

A MULTIVERSE OF CHOICE

You might be thinking, *Yeah, okay. So what?*

But it's important to remember that the nearly limitless choice of information and entertainment we now take for granted is, in fact, something that's erupted in the course of our lifetimes. If we limit the scope of change to just *this millennium,* it's staggering to think of what didn't even exist as recently as 1999: smartphones, social media, YouTube, streaming music and video. In the span of a quarter century—a historical blink—*everything* has changed. And it continues to change.

The four TV channels I had as a kid are nothing compared to the functionally limitless content opportunities a five-year-old today can find via an iPad in her lap. And the power of those personal devices is staggering. According to ZME Science, an Apple iPhone—even an older one—is millions of times more powerful than the mainframe computers NASA used to guide astronauts to the moon in 1969. "You wouldn't be wrong in saying an iPhone could be used to guide 120,000,000 Apollo-era spacecraft to the moon, all at the same time," engineer Tibi Puiu reported.[1]

In high school, I would have had to go to a big library in another city and dig through who knows how much of a card catalog to find that quote. Today, it took me about fifteen seconds—just another bit of proof of how amazingly capable and powerful the technology in our pockets is.

WITH GREAT POWER . . .

In the span of fifty years, we've gone from garage-sized computers to pocket-sized devices that, quite literally, put the sum total of human knowledge and content in the palms of our hands. Perhaps it's no wonder we're on our screens a lot. There's a lot to see.

But as a certain Uncle Ben of a certain friendly neighborhood Spider-Man once famously observed, "With great power comes great responsibility."

Sometimes that responsibility—to help our kids navigate this ever-expanding universe of content and entertainment—can feel overwhelming. As a parent of three teenagers, I feel that reality keenly. It often seems as if my kids are one step ahead of me in terms of encountering what's out there in the digital realm and understanding clearly how to use technology to get there.

The temptation is to do one of two things: to batten down the hatches, lock the digital doors, and do our best to make sure those hermetically sealed portals stay shut. Or we may be tempted to do just the opposite: toss up our hands in frustration and capitulation. *Well, it doesn't matter what we do*, we'll rationalize. *They're going to do exactly what they want online anyway.*

I understand both those temptations. But neither harsh legalism nor exhausted license can effectively equip our children to navigate the real world. To do that, they need our help defining a middle path of meaningful, thoughtful *intentionality*, *engagement*, and *conversation*. Once we understand what that approach looks like for our families, we can establish *boundaries* that aren't harsh or draconian but rather are healthy, life-giving limits that can protect while still offering guidance and direction.

Intentionality

The word *intentionality* turns up a lot these days. Whether in business books, church, or content related to spiritual growth, the importance of being intentional cannot be overstated.

I think intentionality becomes even more critical the more options we have. We—and our children—are absolutely bombarded with options and opportunities with regard to how we invest our time, money, and relational energy.

In his book *7 Traits of Effective Parenting*, Focus on the Family Vice President of Parenting Danny Huerta defines *intentionality* as "knowing what you want to do to make each day count in your child's life and in your opportunity to be transformed."[2]

I like that definition. *Knowing* requires effort and planning; being intentional isn't something that just accidentally happens on its own. Instead, we order and structure our lives so that we can effectively pursue a desired outcome. We embrace discipline and shared values to reinforce what's most important to us: our relationships with each other (especially our family) and with God.

Although she was talking very specifically about discipline as a writer, author Annie Dillard beautifully described in her book *The Writing Life* the kind of deliberate purpose and structure that intentionality can give to our lives:

> How we spend our days is, of course, how we spend
> our lives. What we do with this hour, and that one,
> is what we are doing. A schedule defends from
> chaos and whim. It is a net for catching days. It is a
> scaffolding on which a worker can stand and labor
> with both hands at sections of time. A schedule is a
> mock-up of reason and order—willed, faked, and so
> brought into being; it is a peace and a haven set into

the wreck of time; it is a lifeboat on which you find yourself, decades later, still living.[3]

I confess I'm not a particularly disciplined person by nature. I'm curious, and I love following ideas to see where they lead. Curiosity and wonder are good things. But pair curiosity with the internet in the absence of discipline, and you've got a never-ending rabbit hole into "the wreck of time," as Dillard put it.

That's how an hour gets eaten up by Facebook here, and two hours get consumed by TikTok there, and even more hours evaporate when we spontaneously decide to binge-watch four episodes of a new show we just discovered on Netflix. If that can happen to us as *adults*, how much more are our *kids* susceptible to being swept down this perpetual river of content, often to destinations unknown?

But how do we begin to become more intentional about our—and our kids'—entertainment, media, and screen engagement?

One big step toward this goal, I'd argue, is as simple as it is profound: We must make a fundamental shift from *passive consumption* of entertainment to *active choices* about what we're engaging with and why.

"I just want to veg out" is an expression we've all probably used at some point. And what that looks like will be different from one person to the next. But essentially what it means is two things: We don't want to have to think, and we want to be entertained.

After a long day—or week—at work, an entitlement

mentality can creep in. *I've worked hard*, we might say. *I deserve some downtime with no one asking me to do or think about anything.* It's a kind of willful rebellion against responsibility of all kinds.

For me, vegging out might mean mindlessly surfing through internet sites I like. For my wife, it might mean watching a Hallmark movie.

Now, there's nothing necessarily wrong with either of those pursuits. What's potentially a problem, though, is our attitude: *I deserve space to relax, be entertained, and not have to think.* That attitude is utterly passive and consumption oriented. Instead of thinking thoughtfully about how we might relax, we simply turn the TV on and turn our brains off.

That behavior is self-reinforcing, isn't it? The more I look for some kind of rest and relaxation, the less I want to do anything else. If my children want to talk but I'm staring at my phone, what message does it send to them when I sigh and put it down in exasperation? The message is clear: My passive relaxation is more important than my relationship with my kids, and seeking escape through technology and entertainment is something of a twenty-first-century "unalienable right." To the extent that this is true of us, it will absolutely be true of our children and their habits in this area as well.

Now, the point here isn't to say that you can't watch a movie or TV show to relax. The problem comes when doing this becomes an automatic, unconscious habit—not something we intentionally or purposefully choose, but something we do reflexively in a vain attempt to escape life and its constant pressures and pains.

Having said that, I'm not suggesting we beat ourselves up (at least not too much). Rather, embracing intentionality means growing in self-awareness about our—and our children's—media-related habits. We can do that by asking ourselves (and, again, our families) some basic questions:

- *How do I like to relax?*
- *Do I tend to use entertainment to try to zone out after a hard day or week?*
- *Does this attitude ever feel kind of empty, as though I've just wasted a couple of hours?*
- *How much do I think about my entertainment choices before I make them? How much do I think about what I've watched or engaged in afterward?*

Changing habits in this area—like changing anything we recognize as unhealthy or out of balance—isn't an overnight process. But it begins with that moment of self-awareness and recognition of patterns we need to adjust. We'll talk more about making those changes throughout the balance of this book.

Engagement

Intentionality goes hand in hand with our next area of emphasis: *engagement*. Engagement builds on that active posture of intentionality. When we engage, we roll up our sleeves and get to work understanding two important and interconnected areas: the entertainment content our kids encounter and how it might influence them.

Admittedly, with so much stuff happening in the broad realms of entertainment and technology these days, it can feel overwhelming at times to keep up. That said, one of the glorious things about the internet is that learning about something your kids are suddenly buzzing about isn't as hard as it used to be. Is your daughter listening to Taylor Swift's new album on Spotify? Simply doing a search on "Taylor Swift new album lyrics" will likely bring up everything you need to know (as will checking *Plugged In*'s detailed review, of course).

Recently I picked up my teenage daughter from school, and her phone made a chiming alert sound on the way home that I hadn't heard before. Like one of Pavlov's famously conditioned dogs responding to the sound of a bell, she quickly reached for her phone and posed for a spontaneous selfie right there in the car.

"What are you doing?" I asked.

She told me that she was doing her daily BeReal selfie. I wasn't familiar with that app, so she explained that it prompts users to post a picture once a day, wherever they are, within two minutes, tallied by a countdown that commences as soon as the user gets the notification.

When we got home, I got my own phone out to do some further digging. You can almost always do a search on whatever you're looking for plus the words "parents' guide" to at least start your exploration of what you need to know. I did that and quickly found information giving me the basics on BeReal. Turns out it was designed to combat some of the biggest issues with social media. There's no "like" button, for instance, so kids aren't tempted to judge how good or bad a particular post is based on numerical feedback. Nor are there any filters that enable users to doctor pictures to make them look better. I liked the fact that, observationally, my daughter was on and off in about a minute. No endless scrolling through TikTok or Instagram feeds.

Armed with that information, I went back and asked my daughter what she thought about the app and how she was using it. That led to a bigger conversation about social media in general and how she and her friends used this and other platforms.

So that's one half of the engagement equation: growing in our understanding of what our kids are interested in and spending time with via their screens. The other half involves engaging with our kids enough to know their particular personalities and how various kinds of entertainment and content impact them. Which means we need to become students of our children.

I once reviewed the movie *A Dog's Purpose* for *Plugged In*. The story involved the life of a dog whose personality jumped from one dog to another when each canine reached the end of its life. Essentially, it was portraying something very close to reincarnation. But other than that worldview concern, which I felt my kids and I could talk through and maybe even have a nice theological conversation about, there wasn't anything in the movie that I felt would be super-problematic for them. So the next weekend we went to see the movie at our local dollar theater.

When we got done, I expected a lot of laughs and smiles

from my kids as we talked through the various dogs' antics. But I noticed that my youngest daughter was very quiet. I suspected that maybe the fact that several dogs died in the movie might have been harder on her little heart than I'd anticipated (I believe she was seven years old when we saw the film). So I asked if that was making her sad.

"No, Daddy. That's not it." She paused, then looked at me with concern in her eyes: "Daddy, is our house going to burn down?"

It took me a second to connect the dots and figure out why she was asking a question that seemed completely out of the blue. And then I remembered: In the movie, the young protagonist's house is accidentally destroyed in a fire. It's a dramatic and tragic scene (though no one is ultimately injured). Still, it wasn't something I would have flagged ahead of time as potentially problematic. Yet it was suddenly very clear that this possibility was troubling my daughter much more than the thought of dogs dying and being reincarnated.

"No, honey, our house isn't going to burn down," I tried to reassure her.

But she wasn't having any of it.

"How do you *know*? Can you *promise* our house won't catch on fire? You can't control that."

Well, friends, she was right. And she had me cornered. "You're right, dear. I can't promise that," I said. "All I can say is that it's *unlikely* our house will burn down. But if that *did* happen, we would have to trust God, together, with that loss. It would be hard, but He'd help us get through."

While she didn't really like my answer, it did help her

disconnect from the anxiety that the scene had unexpectedly created for her.

That moment illustrates why it's important not only to know our kids' interests but to also know *them*—especially what their unique trigger points and particularities are. My older two kids had no problem at all with that scene. But my youngest did, and it was a poignant reminder that I needed to think ahead of time about anything in a movie that she might feel anxious about in the real world.

Engagement, then, looks both ways: at our kids *and* at the things they're interested in. Then it dives into understanding how the entertainment they're interested in may be influencing their hearts. Engagement also leads to the next foundational principle when it comes to equipping our kids to think critically about entertainment and technological access to it: *conversation*.

Conversation

So far in this book, we've looked at protecting and guiding our families through the potential minefields of entertainment. But if there's one concept that might just be the linchpin for everything we'll deal with, I'd humbly suggest that it might be conversation.

Conversation, of course, means talking. I know that's basic and self-evident. But let's face it—our first impulse as parents often doesn't involve talking about our kids' entertainment and screen interests. Let me illustrate.

A while back, my kids were talking about some of the songs on their respective playlists while we were all in the car. I pride myself on keeping lines of communication pretty open with my three teens. I feel like I know what they're interested in. But I was totally caught off guard when my middle child mentioned that she had Katy Perry's hit song "California Gurls" on her list.

That's when Dad. Went. *OFF.*

"*What?*" I practically yelled. (And she would say I *did* yell.) "Katy Perry? I don't want you listening to her. The messages in that song are terrible!" I went on like that for maybe a couple more "I don't want you listening to that garbage" kinds of sentences. And when my spontaneous little rant was done . . . total silence from my daughter. She sat like a stone. And despite a bit of encouragement, I couldn't get her to say anything. She completely shut down, conversationally, relationally, and emotionally.

It wasn't my finest moment as a parent. Nor did my response, in any way, constitute conversation. It was, as I characterized it, a rant.

Over the next couple of days, I had to do some damage control with my daughter to repair the rupture in our relationship. I let her know that while I had some concerns about the lyrics of that song—and with Katy Perry's work in general—I had not acted in a *respectful* way that would have invited a deeper conversation about why that particular song might not be the best choice.

Conversation—real conversation—requires trust and respect. It requires a safe space to share ideas without fear of being shut down or dismissed or shamed. I didn't *talk* with her about Katy Perry. I *told* her. It was a one-way road, and conversationally, I'd run her over. So why on earth would she trust me in similar conversations in the future?

Those two values—trust and respect—are foundational building blocks for our relationships with our kids, and they're absolutely necessary if we hope to have ongoing conversations with them about media. There will certainly be times when we need to say no. And some of what they're interested in may well be beyond the pale in terms of content (I'll share another such story later). But even in these cases, as our children move from their tweens to their teens, our goal is to cultivate conversation instead of issuing edicts. Because before we know it, they'll be making their own entertainment choices. And our little talks could impact those choices.

Conversation—real dialogue—with our kids builds relationship and keeps the door open to helping them think about the deeper issues they may be encountering in entertainment. The goal in our discussions is to model for our kids how to think about the ideas that are coming at them through images and words.

Another thing to keep in mind regarding conversation is that it can happen at any point: before, during, or after you or your kids engage with some form of entertainment.

For example, my oldest son recently came to me and said that some of his friends were getting together to watch the 2000 movie *American Psycho*.

As of this writing, my son is sixteen, and he's a junior in high school. We're giving him more leeway now with regard to his TV viewing, gaming, and music choices.

That said, *American Psycho* remains one of the most

graphically explicit and problematic films of the past twenty-five years. Whatever kinds of nasty content you can think of, it turns up in this movie. So I said, "Son, you know that we give you quite a bit of freedom to make your own decisions. But this is a case where we need to say no. There's a lot of sex, violence, and profanity in this movie."

He was disappointed, but he was willing to submit to our decision.

"I understand," he said. "It's okay."

I think he was able to respond that way in part because we talk about his choices and often say yes, even when there are issues we need to talk through. He also understood that we knew what was in the movie; he knew we weren't just having a knee-jerk reaction to something we didn't truly understand. So he didn't push back but accepted our no in this case.

On the other hand, it doesn't always work out quite as smoothly.

I found out from him later on that he'd watched every episode of, gulp, *Breaking Bad*, a TV-MA–rated show that also has a ton of disturbing content. Again, his friends had been the ones who'd turned him on to the show. (Peer influence remains a perennial issue.) There was nothing I could do about it, no way I could make him *unsee* what he'd seen.

I could have disciplined him harshly or gone off like I did with my poor daughter regarding Katy Perry. But my internal response was *Well, it already happened*. It was a little like a fender bender or a winter storm or a health problem: I just had to deal with the circumstances in front of me.

So I told him, "I'm not thrilled that you watched a

TV-MA–rated show without talking to me about it first. But let's talk about it now."

That led to a long conversation in which I peppered him with questions:

"What was appealing about the show?"

"What cautionary lessons did it teach?"

"What images or content bothered you or stayed with you?"

I also told him that I didn't want him to watch any more shows with a mature rating without talking to me first.

Was that the right approach? I can't say for sure. Some parents might have been more disciplinarian than we were. Others might have blown it off. But we tried to walk a middle path between those extremes while talking all the way.

I could give more such examples. But I think you get the point: Especially as our kids move through their teen years, we want to cultivate conversation grounded in trust and respect. We aren't perfect, so we may not always get it right—as my own illustrations have, I hope, demonstrated. But if our kids know that we're more invested in our relationship with them than we are simply trying to enforce rules, it will pay dividends in our connection with them as they move toward adulthood.

Boundaries

Those dividends might be the most obvious when it comes to a subject that, frankly, most of us probably aren't that crazy about—whether we're parents, kids, or in some other season of life. I'm talking about boundaries, of course. Or, put more bluntly, rules. Limitations. Agreements on what's in bounds and what's out of bounds.

Before we dive into some boundaries to consider, let me say that boundaries are hard. By nature, we're talking about putting limits on something we or our kids want to do. It doesn't feel very good. And that can be even more true if you're the only family around who even seems to be thinking about this issue.

I'll also add that, honestly, my family's not great at setting boundaries—maybe because I didn't have very many myself growing up. Some families naturally kind of feel their way through things, while others are naturally disciplined and regimented. We're definitely in the former category, which means that sometimes we've had to adjust our boundaries after the fact.

It's an imperfect process, to be sure. And we can err on either side. That said, prioritizing relationship and communication as we set limits is perhaps even more important than the particular rules and regulations we establish for our children. With that in mind, let's look more deeply at some important categories for boundaries we need to set.

Researchers have repeatedly shown that even if kids naturally seem to push against boundaries, they unconsciously want them. And so do we. When we know where the "fences" in life are, we can live with a sense of security and confidence. But when boundaries are unclear, especially for children, it can create a sense of unease because they don't know where the edge of the proverbial playing field is.

Entire books have been written on the importance of

knowing where our limitations are. For the purposes of entertainment and technology, however, we can focus on four concrete areas as we strive to set appropriate limits that protect our kids and give them an opportunity to flourish in their maturing process:

What content will we engage with?
Where will that happen?
How long will we be engaged with it?
With whom will we do that?

The answers to these four questions will vary depending on a child's maturity and development, and they'll change as kids get older.

What?

When we think about setting limits on entertainment, this is very likely the question that comes to mind first: What is out of bounds? The younger your child is, the longer the list of content concerns you'll likely have that push various forms of entertainment out of bounds. These include obvious issues such as profanity and sexually explicit imagery. But parents will also need to think about issues that are perhaps less clear-cut. What about a story that emphasizes the concept of evolution, or one that delivers an emotional defense for something like euthanasia? (I'm looking at you, *Million Dollar Baby*.)

There are no cookie-cutter, one-size-fits-all answers here. Instead, you'll have to decide which images, ideas, and issues are out of bounds for your children at their varying stages of development.

Where?

At first glance, this question might seem less obvious. Not that long ago, really, the answer *was* obvious: Most entertainment took place where the family TV was. These days, though, anyone with a smartphone or tablet likely has access to a broad range of movies and TV programming, as well as internet-based content on YouTube and social media. Families will need to decide what limits should be placed on devices in bedrooms, especially at night.

Jonathan McKee, author of *Parenting Generation Screen*, strongly advises no phones in kids' bedrooms at night. From social media notifications to video games to pornography use, kids with access to screen devices in their rooms at night risk exposure to harmful content as well as interruptions in healthy nighttime sleep patterns.

How Long?

The American Academy of Child and Adolescent Psychiatry offers detailed screen-time advice for young children:

> Until 18 months of age limit screen use to video chatting along with an adult (for example, with a parent who is out of town). Between 18 and 24 months screen time should be limited to watching educational programming with a caregiver. For children 2–5, limit non-educational screen time

to about 1 hour per weekday and 3 hours on the weekend days. For ages 6 and older, encourage healthy habits and limit activities that include screens.[4]

For many years, the rule of thumb for multiple experts has been two hours of screen time a day, in part because more than that has correlated with unhealthy mental and physical health outcomes, such as anxiety, depression, and obesity, among other things. The problem, however, is that the gap between what's *recommended* and what today's screen-using kids are *actually doing* is enormous. The Common Sense Census reported in 2021 that the average eight- to twelve-year-old spends five hours and thirty-three minutes a day on screens, while thirteen- to eighteen-year-olds use screens eight hours and thirty-nine minutes each day.[5]

If your family's screen-time use is closer to the average than what's recommended, reducing screen time can seem daunting. Chapter 10, "The Reset," offers concrete tips for reducing your family's screen-time usage.

With Whom?

Finally, it's important to consider not only *what*, *where*, and *when* but also *with whom* our kids are engaged in screen use. Are they connecting with others online via FaceTime or another video app? Are they completely isolated in their rooms as they surf TikTok or other social media sites? Are they watching a movie with Mom and Dad in the living room? While being alone with a device isn't necessarily a problem, a family with multiple children who all have their own screens can easily find themselves drifting their separate ways, interacting primarily with their devices instead of with each other.

Setting and maintaining boundaries almost never feels like an easy or fun thing to do. But, as the author of Hebrews wrote, "for the moment all discipline seems painful rather than pleasant, but later it yields the peaceful fruit of righteousness to those who have been trained by it" (Hebrews 12:11, ESV).

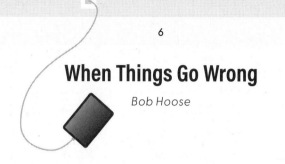

When Things Go Wrong

Bob Hoose

WE JUST TALKED ABOUT putting together an entertainment game plan for you and your kids. And we all know that, if we're going to succeed at anything in our lives, it helps to have a plan.

But here's the thing about plans: They never work perfectly. Ask any head coach in the NFL. Ask any Little League baseball manager. Ask *anyone*—from the city planner to your kid's kindergarten teacher—if they've ever had anything go *exactly* the way they planned it. And if they say they have, well, they're a lot luckier than the rest of us.

If you're coming to this chapter eager to find answers, you're likely in a situation where things are kinda . . . maybe . . . sorta going haywire when it comes to your or your kids' media use. Whatever plan you had—whether it was based on the ground rules we covered or was a plan of your own or was a little of both—just went south.

Perhaps you just found out that your son has been playing a grisly shooter game at a friend's house and now really wants it for Christmas. Or maybe your children went to a sleepover and the host kid's parents let them watch that new slasher movie *I Screamed at What You Did Last Summer*, and nobody in your house is getting a full night's sleep anymore. It could be that you and your spouse are both spending *waaay* too much time on that time-suck called social media. Or maybe it's something as simple as coming to realize that you haven't given your teens much guidance with their media consumption, and that you haven't had much of a plan at all. Now you're worried that their phones might be permanently grafted to their palms.

Whatever your situation, the first step is to pause. Then take a nice, deep breath.

Then consider your particular predicament and look for some commonsense solutions.

And while we're gearing up to do *that*, you should also realize that you're not the hopelessly failed parent you might think you are. The fact is that every parent in the world has gone or will go through similar things—especially in this high-tech, media-driven world we live in. Yep, whether you're a capital-S-wearing Superparent, a lowercase-s-wearing slacker parent, or anything in between, you *will* make mistakes: Your kids will trip up or break the rules, and at some point your family will likely seem on the brink of catastrophe over one dumb choice or another.

And you know what? You're *not* going to find a magic red fix-it button—some simple, cut-and-dried solution that fits everybody. I used to think there was such a thing. Some people will sell you books, videos, and podcasts telling you that a simple solution is yours to be had. But they're wrong. Period.

Every parent and child can respond differently to every idea or situation they're faced with. Why? Because God created us uniquely and wonderfully different. (Perhaps that's also why the Bible is chock-full of far more than just one big Golden Rule.)

What you *can* find—and what you *will* find here—are some suggestions and approaches that can help mitigate the inevitable stumbles that come your way. You can take a look and try some out—like slipping into a pair of new shoes—and see if they fit your family. So let's get our metaphorical shoehorn out and get started.

PARENTING STYLES

The first thing to consider is how you relate and interact with your kids. I start here because our own communication and parenting styles are key to how we connect with our families and fix our problems. In fact, that connection establishes and shapes our kids' morals, values, language, and conduct. That connection also shapes our family *culture*, for lack of a better word.

Researchers have grouped our parenting styles in various ways, but developmental psychologist Diana Baumrind once described four basic parenting categories: neglectful (uninvolved), permissive, authoritarian, and authoritative.[1]

Now, at first glance, those categories all sound as if they might have a few problems. Let's look a little closer.

Neglectful

Neglectful (or uninvolved) parenting is pretty much exactly what it sounds like: Parents stay detached, and kids have very little guidance. This parenting style gives plenty of freedom to kids (and parents, for that matter), and it even tends to make children more resilient and self-sufficient out of necessity. But without parental nurturing and expectations, most kids who grow up under this style of parenting end up having trouble with everything from controlling their tempers to coping with stress and maintaining relationships.

Permissive

These parents can be warm and nurturing, but they keep the rules so light that discipline is rare and expectations tend to be low. Permissive adult figures are more like pals than parents. They want kids to figure life out on their own. To our adult brains, that sounds wise and esteem-building, but unguided kids generally become demanding and impulsive with little self-regulation. Child obesity can be a problem in this camp too.

Authoritarian

This style of parenting is pretty common. It's the ironfisted, less nurturing, my-way-or-the-highway style that brand-new parents often turn to first. Rules are rules, it says. Kids must behave well, it demands. No negotiation!

Now, rules can be good, but standing tall, pointing, and saying no with a commanding voice only works for so long.

I'll raise my hand and admit that I started out with this approach as a first-time dad leaping into the parenting throng. I figured that if I held my kids accountable and taught them well, they'd be better than all those other idiot children in the world. Eventually I saw the error of my ways. My relationship with my firstborn is great now, but her teen years were a rocky road. This overly firm parenting style can often result in kids' struggling with rebellion (uh-huh), poor self-esteem, and an inability to make their own decisions.

Authoritative

This parenting style might *sound* similar to the last one, but there's an important tweak. It's about being an authority figure kids *want* to look to for guidance rather than being someone who *demands* that they do so. Authoritative parenting incorporates the best parts of the permissive and authoritarian approaches and eliminates the problematic bits.

Authoritative parents develop a close, nurturing relationship with their kids while setting clear guidelines and rules. In this case, Mom and Dad also take the time to listen to their kids and explain the rules and reasons for them. Not only can the kids get in on setting their own goals and expectations with this approach, but they also have a clear picture of why discipline is applied when it's necessary.

Sounds like a perfect sweet spot, right? Yep. But getting there also takes time and patience. And it puts the weight of leading by example on your shoulders. That's not always easy when you're in a rush and time is short. But boy is it important. More on why in a bit.

GROUND RULES

If you've got little kids and a permissive parenting style that hasn't been as productive or healthy as it should be, you're in luck: There's still time for you to make some course corrections that will pay dividends in the long run. If, on the other hand, you're a mom or dad with some authoritarian tendencies and a snarling teen who's shut off all communication from their base somewhere on the dark side of the moon, well, you've got some ground to make up.

With that in mind, here are some tiny rules that might help your family take baby steps toward a more productive give-and-take.

Honestly Own It

If you want to make things better with your kids (in any and every area), be honest about that fact. Talk with them about the changes you hope to see in them and in you, and why those changes are important. Then own up to your *own* mistakes.

Yep, it's not just the kids who blow it. And it can be particularly harmful when we cover up one little mistake or two and then compound them into bigger mistakes in the future. Half-truths and manipulation aren't going to cut it if you want lasting change. Modeling a process of everyone admitting mistakes, asking for forgiveness, and making things right is a great foundation to build on at any age.

Live It

If there are changes you want to see in your family and its patterns, you should be the first in line. If, for instance, you want your teens to adjust their social media consumption, movie watching, gaming, and/or phone usage, then you'd better examine your own time in front of screens. The old adage *Do as I say, not as I do* has always been dumb, and it never works. For anybody.

Encourage It

Reinforce the positive things you see your kids doing and the positive changes you see them making. And let them contribute to the process. To take an example: Years ago, when my youngest child was still pretty tiny, she saw me reading a Stephen King novel and came up to say that she thought Daddy shouldn't be reading scary stories. Now, my first thought was to wonder how she knew the book was scary. Unless my wife's bedtime-story-reading regimen had radically changed, we'd never even mentioned Stephen King to our daughters before. But then my second thought was . . . that she was probably right: There likely were other healthier stories I could be reading and thoughts I could be filling my noggin with. So I agreed and put the book aside.

Now, I'm not slamming Stephen King books or fans thereof, but it was a good chance for me to reinforce the idea with my daughter that making wise choices about what we read and play and watch is a smart thing for everybody to do—even daddies. It taught her that she could be discerning about what's good and not so good.

Believe it or not, kids of any age are always watching what we do and following after us. Frankly, you're the biggest influencer in your children's lives, even when it doesn't seem that way.

Listen for It

We parents tend to talk a lot. Sure, we've got all those *brilliant* parenty things to share, but sometimes the best way to do that is by asking questions and really listening to the answers kids give us.

For instance, have you ever thought about what makes a great movie? We've got so many films these days that seek to drive home a particular social, environmental, or political point by screaming out a message over and over. And those are usually the most boring, tedious pics at the movie house. But when a well-made story draws you in and asks poignant questions, that's when your brain starts to mull things over in earnest. That's exactly what you can do with your kids.

In the previous chapter, Adam talked about how important conversation is when putting together a game plan. But guess what? Conversation is a pretty good fix-it tool too—just try a little bit of conversational duct tape when your plan takes a hit or you've made some mistakes along the way.

Take the time to sit over a soda with your kids or go out for a walk and talk through any problems or concerns they may have. Pay attention. And then let the things they're talking about inform some *questions* you can ask rather than *answers* you want to give. Remember, your kids need a safe space, and they need to know you're listening. Asking questions instead of injecting answers might feel like a waste of time if you *have* all the answers—but your child or teen won't think so. A well-thought-through question can get kids thinking about the right and wrong of things. It can start them asking questions themselves. And rather than you blathering on, the two of you end up discovering some of those brilliant kernels of life wisdom *together*.

Walk It

And while I'm talking about taking a walk, you might want to think about opting for more activity in your family life. Instead of always hopping in the car to get somewhere—with passengers young and old glued to their cell-phone screens— take the time to walk there if possible. Ride bikes to school, to the park, or for a coffee. Hey, what about getting a dog? Studies have shown that becoming more active with your family contributes to better health and a closer family unit. And doing all that with your nose in a phone is nearly impossible. (I mean, dogs *hate* those things.)

Love It

Of course, what I'm saying here is that you should be mindful of *loving* your kids in the midst of the changes or problems you encounter. This is especially true if you're just starting to get your family's entertainment habits under control and are facing resistance. Hey, that's bound to happen, right? You wouldn't like it if I came over to your house and told you to quit watching reality TV, would you—even if you knew I was right? And for kids who might not be so sure you're right, putting a game plan in place (or putting a little extra oomph into an existing game plan) will require tact, patience, and most important, a lot of love. That also goes for when your kids stumble and break whatever entertainment rules you have in place.

Change is never easy, but reasoned, loving explanations go much further than demands. If somebody has messed up, don't start pounding the table and rending your garments about all the ways that life as we know it has been destroyed. Walk through things calmly with that sense of honesty and forgiveness I mentioned earlier.

Note that I'm not saying that you should *ignore* any broken rules or idiotic choices made with a screen. We all know there are some potentially big rules to break and colossally dumb choices to make on that front! I'm just saying that a functioning family loves its way through big problems.

Go Forth

Now, if you're suddenly sitting up and saying "Hold on! Everything you're suggesting here is about *me* needing to change," well, you've grabbed the proverbial brass ring. 'Cause that's *exactly* what I'm saying. Every jot and tittle of the process of making your family stronger and healthier with their consumption of media—and on every other front of life—falls to you.

You'll also notice, I'm sure, that you haven't found a single recommendation here about how to lock your kids out of their smartphones, or how to construct a media contract that will hold all your family members accountable, or how to convince people to go out and burn their gaming consoles (pant, pant, pant), or *anything* like that!

Once again you are completely correct. And here's why. None of those control-focused choices or routines work for everybody. They might help some, but not everybody. Every kid's personality is different, and temperaments can vary like the seasons. Sometimes your likes and temperament instantly click with your child, and sometimes not. You can be fastidious and rule driven and have a kid who's completely oblivious to the idea of even putting their clothes in a drawer rather than in a pile on the floor.

It all comes down to you and how you and your family communicate. That's a huge job. But it's also the *only* thing you can totally control: how you react, how much you invest and give. It's up to you to be discerning when it comes to foul movies, gross games, destructive social media, and nasty music. And it's up to you to get involved in all those areas with your kids—listening, playing, and watching with them—and then gently teaching them to be discerning too.

I've casually referenced my kids at different points in this chapter. And the fact is that they were all completely different. It was up to me to approach them where they were. For my eldest, it required backing off, apologizing, and starting again. For my middle child, it meant developing a new language and connecting with him over something he passionately loved—in his case, the world of video games. And with my youngest, it was all about long walks, deep talks, and digging for those kernels of mutually sought wisdom.

Your family may require something completely different

when it comes to the media they consume, how they'll process it, and how to decipher how it impacts them. But it all begins with your ability, Mom and Dad, to reach out, put an arm around your child, experience things, and talk it through. That's why *your* time, *your* changes, and *your* choices make all the difference in the world. And *that's* what you can do now.

Playing the Long Game

Adam R. Holz

"BUT WHY?" my son asked. *"Why* can't I watch Marvel movies? All my friends are *already* watching them."

And there it was: the one question every child at some point wields angrily like a crowbar. Naturally, as parents, we're tempted to answer these questions with a couple of well-worn answers we probably heard (and hated) from our own parents. One, *Because I said so,* and two, *If all your friends jumped off a cliff, would you jump off a cliff too?*

Okay, when the above conversation happened with my son, who was ten or eleven at the time, I didn't *actually* reach for either of those ready-made parental clichés, tempting as they might have been. Instead, I reminded him that his mother and I didn't think he was old enough for the content in those films. And I tried to help him understand our reasons for saying no to something that it seemed like every other family had said yes to.

As parents, we know that this moment is coming. We know that helping our kids grow up in general, and dealing with entertainment choices in particular, will likely make us the bad guy in their eyes at some point. As a natural-born people pleaser, I *hate* being the bad guy, even though I know it's the right thing sometimes. Being the bad guy for good reasons is an important part of my job as a dad. But it can be hard, especially when our kids keep jamming and wiggling that rhetorical crowbar ever more deeply into our arguments.

That story from my own parental experience illustrates a core question when it comes to helping our children grow in their ability to make wise entertainment choices on their own: How do we know when to say no? How do we know when to say yes? And how do we navigate the rocky, sometimes unclear territory between those two answers?

FROM NO TO YES

When it comes to shaping our children's entertainment and technology engagement, some things feel fairly self-evident—or at least they *should* to mature and healthy parents. Obviously, we're not going to let our kids watch R-rated movies when they're five years old. We're not letting them play *Call of Duty* when they're in kindergarten. We're not signing them up for TikTok in second grade. Those examples are an automatic no because the gap between that content and their maturity is, I hope, completely self-evident.

On the other end of the age spectrum, though, most parents hope their kids will have the tools they need to make good decisions on their own by the time they leave home. We want them to be able to think critically, to recognize when something is potentially harmful, and to be able to enjoy entertainment and technology without drowning in it or being captivated by an unbiblical worldview.

It's that gap in between where things get a bit murky though, right? How *do* we get from point A to point B? How do we gradually shift from an age-appropriate stance of protection and avoiding problematic content to wisely teaching and guiding our kids to evaluate entertainment for themselves by the time they're young adults?

That might seem like a daunting task, maybe even kind of impossible. But it doesn't have to be.

AVOIDANCE, CAUTION, AND DIALOGUE

In his 2000 book *Reel Spirituality: Theology and Film in Dialogue*, Fuller Theological Seminary professor Robert K. Johnston develops a very detailed grid (drawing from Richard Niebuhr's work *Christ and Culture*) for thinking through how we might approach film (and, by extension, entertainment in general) from a Christian perspective.

With a nod to Johnston's thinking, I'm going to borrow a small portion of his grid here to talk about how we as parents might think about three ways Christians can relate to popular culture: *avoidance, caution,* and *dialogue.*[1]

Those words might seem concrete and self-explanatory, but let's unpack them anyway.

Avoidance, caution, and dialogue represent three different responses to things our families or our children encounter in culture. When faced with a choice about whether we're going to watch a particular movie, for instance, we can simply avoid it; we can move forward in caution, knowing that we might at any point have to turn it off; or we can actively and intentionally watch it and then talk about the issues it presents.

Let's dive into this continuum of overlapping approaches, including when we implement them and what that looks like in action.

Avoidance

How do you respond to the word *avoidance*? It's not the most inviting word, right? Why? Because it obviously implies that we're saying no to something. And if there's a word that our popular culture hates, it's the word *no*.

We live in a world that wants us to embrace the ideas, attitudes, and images being thrust at us from every direction through entertainment, advocacy, and advertising. No one wants to be seen as embodying the stodgy attitudes of yesteryear, being an "old fuddy-duddy" or a "Goody-Two-Shoes" or a "stick-in-the-mud." (Never mind that most kids today have never even *heard* those phrases.) Instead, we hear commercial catchphrases like *No rules, just right* and *Just do it*. We see bumper stickers with different iterations of *No limits* and *No fear*.

To suggest, then, that there *are* limits and boundaries and ideas that are out of bounds for our families' entertainment choices is a fundamentally countercultural choice these days.

As I talked about earlier, I'm pretty sure we were the last family in my son's peer group to greenlight Marvel movies. So I had to help him understand our decision. (I'll say more about that in a moment.)

As Christian parents, however, we understand and believe that we're strangers in a strange land, making our way through a world—and its accompanying entertainment landscape— that embraces different values and understandings than our own. In Romans 12:1-2, for instance, the apostle Paul contrasted two different ways of life: being conformed to worldly patterns or being transformed by the renewal of our minds when we immerse our hearts in truth.

Living as followers of Christ in the world, then, means that we sometimes say no to popular entertainment that others are embracing. That's going to be true for us as we guide our children, and it remains true for us as adults as well. Sometimes a given movie or TV show deserves the answer no . . . for everyone.

With my son, saying no meant helping him understand that those Marvel movies had some problems I didn't want to expose him to yet. The primary area I was concerned about was the profanity: Most superhero movies push close to the limit of what's allowed in a PG-13 film. But I was similarly concerned about the violence (obviously a big issue in superhero flicks) and the occasional sensual or suggestive themes and scenes some Marvel movies include.

"Okay, Dad," he said finally, a bit sullenly.

I felt bad about putting this wall between my son and something he really wanted to engage with. But even though saying no felt like the end of the world for a few minutes, it wasn't.

Especially when our kids are younger, we should say no more than we say yes in almost every area of their lives, and this includes the entertainment arena. Just as we might say no to a three-year-old reaching for a stove burner (whether it's on or not), we say no to young kids when it comes to entertainment that's just too mature for them or that they wouldn't understand. We know as parents that a show might be too scary for them, or too profane, or too violent. We know they're not prepared to deal with some movies' content issues. We know that the younger our kids are, the more sponge-like their minds are and the more tender their souls can be. We say no for their own good, even if they don't understand why.

So we need to, as much as we can, help them understand.

To combat the inevitable frustration that comes with a no, we need to go beyond the *I said so* response. We need to do two things: Help them understand that our decisions are based on our Christian convictions and identify positive alternatives where we can say yes.

Let me give an example of the former. My family enjoys the long-running reality TV competition *America's Got Talent*. I'd say, offhandedly, that perhaps 80 percent of the acts are family friendly. From singing and dancing to ventriloquism and animal gimmicks to card tricks and fun with swords, the range of talent on display is diverse and inspiring.

Every now and then, though, there's an act that sprints over the line in some way.

A while back, for instance, a medium was going to perform a live séance on the show. I told my family that we weren't going to watch this act, and we turned the TV off. I then explained to my kids what a medium and a séance were, and how they involved an attempt to contact spirits of the dead. We talked about how both the Old and New Testaments prohibit such things, and we then read and talked through the apostle Paul's description in Ephesians 6 of the spiritual war raging around us.

Now, I'd be exaggerating if I claimed that as a family we're always that intentional or spiritual when it comes to the stuff we see together on TV. We're not. But here was a clear case where avoidance was the right response: This particular act was clearly against what Scripture teaches.

When a stance of avoidance is, ahem, unavoidable, my wife and I also look for positive and fun alternatives to engage with our kids in other ways.

For many years, my son and I read books together. It started when he was perhaps six or seven and I read to him about a chapter a night from C. S. Lewis's *The Magician's Nephew* (the prelude to *The Lion, the Witch, and the Wardrobe* in The Chronicles of Narnia series).

That book launched us into enjoying fantasy novels together. Over the next six or seven years, I read to him at bedtime as we made our way through more than twenty-five novels. Some of them were faith focused. Some of them weren't. But that experience together was one we both looked forward to for many years, and one that I think helped soften the disappointment when my wife and I did say no in other areas (like to superhero movies).

Sometimes such activities might *literally* take the place of a bit of entertainment that you determine your kids should avoid. Say your daughter wants to stream a problematic Disney movie. Why not say "No, I'm afraid that movie's out of bounds for now . . . but why don't we play a game instead?"

This kind of intentional engagement, even when we say no, can help keep our kids from becoming exasperated by a constant chorus of them. I believe this is at least in part what Paul was talking about when he wrote, "Fathers, do not exasperate your children; instead, bring them up in the training and instruction of the Lord" (Ephesians 6:4). Paul understood, I believe, that when we harshly say no to our kids without teaching them to understand the rationale and foundation for our decisions, it can lead to hard-heartedness and rebellion.

Caution

As our kids get older, those automatic *no* responses become less clear, and we may begin to consider saying yes to choices that might once have been obviously out of bounds.

In our family, some of those choices included PG-13 movie franchises such as *The Lord of the Rings* and *Star Wars*. I think we held out on the Marvel movies for my son until he was around twelve or so (still a bit shy of the thirteen-year-old threshold recommended by the Motion Picture Association).

The cautionary approach, as the word *caution* implies,

is somewhere between yes and no, at least initially. For us as parents, it requires doing our homework and thinking through entertainment choices ahead of time.

That will likely involve several potential steps. First, it can mean checking a website such as *Plugged In* to get a sense of what the issues might be in a particular movie, show, game, or song. Armed with that important information, we can form an opinion of whether it's something our kids can deal with.

Next, if you still have questions, it may require you to see something ahead of time. When there are significant questions about a story that might be right on the edge, previewing it beforehand will give you firsthand knowledge about where a given piece of entertainment falls on the yes/no spectrum.

This is also a good time to note a couple of important things about the rating systems in play for various forms of entertainment, in terms of both the usefulness and the limitations of those systems. The Motion Picture Association (the advisory body behind the familiar rating system that puts the *G*, *PG*, and other ratings on films) relies on a group of parents who have a list of standards involving nudity, profanity, and violence that theoretically enable them to rate movies consistently.[2] That said, the list is also pretty arbitrary when it comes to where some of those lines are drawn. A PG-13 movie can have one or two f-words, for example, but there's no parallel limit on the number of s-words. Similar rules regarding sexuality and violent acts also come into play that separate PG from PG-13 and R ratings.

Similarly, it's also important to note that sensitivity to certain content has changed over time. A PG rating for a movie in the late seventies or early eighties might include nudity, drug use, or violence that would almost certainly earn an R-rating today. *Kramer vs. Kramer*, *The Beastmaster*, and *Smokey and the Bandit Part 3* all include rather shocking amounts of nudity, while violent films such as *Gremlins* and *Indiana Jones and the Temple of Doom* were in part responsible for the creation of the PG-13 rating in 1984.

Even if we're not talking about older films with problems that extreme, you still might be surprised by how much profanity and sexual innuendo there are in old "classics" like *Ghostbusters*, *Back to the Future*, or even *The Goonies*. With regard to the latter, my wife picked it up on DVD years ago (pre-streaming) and brought it home for us to watch as a family. I said, "Well, we can try. But I guarantee that there's more stuff here than you remember." We made it about five minutes before the barrage of s-words prompted us to turn it off.

As for ratings in other forms of media, the Entertainment Software Rating Board likewise uses an independent group of content raters who give ratings for video games. But, notably, TV and music ratings don't come from such a third-party board. Rather, they are both *self-rated* by those producing them, which makes the rating systems significantly more prone to inconsistencies—as well as to understating the amount of inappropriate content present. (I don't think we'd want most of our kids to grade themselves on how well they're doing in algebra. Personally, I think the same can be said for allowing networks and streaming services to grade what shows of theirs are suitable for our children.)

For those reasons, the ratings for all these forms of entertainment should be viewed as a *starting point* rather than the *final word* on whether or not something is appropriate for your children.

But problematic content isn't the only thing we need to be cautious about. In addition to familiarizing ourselves with what to expect before watching something, we need to be students of our children and know what might be upsetting to them.

I mentioned in chapter 5 that my youngest daughter was really bothered by a movie in which a house burned down. That was an important moment where I began to see her unique vulnerabilities and how those vulnerabilities connected with the stories we watched on-screen. But it wasn't the last such moment.

A couple of years later, we were staying in a rental condo for our kids' state swim meet. It wasn't super fancy, but they did have a nice selection of movies to watch. We looked through the stack and ultimately selected the 1989 film *The Bear*, which I had distant memories of. It was a nature movie, so how bad could it be, right?

It was as if I'd never seen an animal movie before. After all, what usually happens in these stories? Someone dies. Usually a parent. Often a mother.

And so it was here. A mama bear is killed by a rockslide in the movie's first three or so minutes, leaving her poor little cub orphaned. By now I knew enough to at least consider how it might be influencing my youngest daughter. I glanced over at her, and she was totally rigid, a tear streaming down her face. And . . . that was that.

Not only did we turn off the movie—literally five minutes into it—we spent the rest of the afternoon doing impromptu counseling for my traumatized daughter. After all, if a freak rockslide could kill a bear, couldn't something accidental kill *her* mom too? The tears didn't stop flowing for quite a while, though eventually I think we spent some time praying and asking God to help us trust Him with anxiety and fear about outcomes we can't control.

Once again, it reminded me that even when we're being intentional and trying to make good media choices, we may run into surprises that force us to quickly rethink our decisions.

Sometimes, even when we've done our homework and proceed cautiously, we may still have issues related to images or ideas to talk about with our kids that we never saw coming. So when you say yes to something—even when it looks like it'll be just fine—be mindful. If you can watch the movie or show with your kids, do so. Watch them as they watch. Be there to answer any questions or offer reassurance. Always be aware of opportunities to talk, even if it means pausing the movie for a moment. And if you can't be in the same room when they're watching, let them know you're always there and are always happy to talk through what they've seen.

Which brings us to the third way we can approach popular culture.

Dialogue

This word does double duty here. We want to have dialogue not only with each other but also, in a way, with the entertainment we're consuming as we help our kids learn to think critically and biblically about what they consume. We want to teach our kids to ask hard questions of the movies they watch. We don't literally talk *to* the screen, but we do want to talk *through* what it shows us. We should never let our entertainment dominate the conversation. We've got to talk back.

With the first two approaches to entertainment—avoidance and caution—our focus as parents is on protecting our kids from images and ideas that could potentially harm their development. As they progress through the teen years, though, our goal is to move toward equipping them to know how to deal with such content when they do come into contact with it later on. We're teaching them to have a conversation—with us, with others, with themselves, with God—about the nature of what they're choosing. Our end game here is to help our kids think clearly about and, hopefully, cultivate a spiritual sensitivity that enables them to recognize what they need to say no to without us being there to help them do that.

So how does that happen? I'd like to suggest that there are two overarching elements in play: developing a biblical grid for evaluating entertainment and asking questions that help our kids consider how entertainment might be affecting them.

A Biblical Grid

There are many passages of Scripture we could focus on to help us develop a biblical grid for wise entertainment choices, but let me focus on five: Ephesians 5:15-17; 1 Corinthians 6:12 and 10:23; Proverbs 4:23; and Psalm 16:11.

In his letter to the church at Ephesus, Paul talks a lot about new believers' identity in Christ, especially in the first three chapters of that book. The last three chapters focus on taking those theological truths and applying them practically to life. Smack-dab in the middle of that second section, Paul admonishes his readers, "Be very careful, then, how you live—not as unwise, but as wise, making the most of every opportunity, because the days are evil. Therefore do not be foolish, but understand what the Lord's will is" (Ephesians 5:15-17).

A literal translation of the exhortation "be very careful" is "see clearly how you walk around." The King James Version translates that phrase "walk circumspectly" (as we discussed in chapter 1). In other words, pay attention to the world around you. As for the evil Paul mentions here, he isn't talking about the kind of stuff we might consider evil, like mass murders and ruthless dictators. Rather, he is talking about the world's system of thought being arrayed in opposition to a biblical worldview and understanding.

Ephesus, you see, was a spiritually diverse, syncretistic center of commerce and government in Asia Minor. It was also home to the world's biggest amphitheater at the time (seating fifty thousand people) and the Temple of Artemis, one of the seven wonders of the ancient world. It was a cosmopolitan marketplace of competing ideas about life, love, truth, and reality. Paul urged the Ephesians to recognize those worldly ideas and compare them carefully with their newfound faith in Christ.

We might paraphrase his teaching and apply it to our modern discussion of entertainment choices with this question: *Is this entertainment bending me toward the world or toward God's way of seeing the world?*

Paul wrote something similar in his letters to the believers in the city of Corinth, which was, like Ephesus, another swirling world of philosophy, religious expressions, and worldliness. Twice in 1 Corinthians, he quoted a local proverb and then contrasted it with biblical thinking about its effectiveness for life guidance: "'I have the right to do anything,' you say—but not everything is beneficial. 'I have the right to do anything'—but I will not be mastered by anything" (1 Corinthians 6:12).

In an earlier chapter, Kennedy Unthank referenced Paul's stream of thought, and it feels especially appropriate when we're talking about this concept of dialogue with our kids. Paul himself thought it so important that he returned to this phrase four chapters later, repeating the same idea with a slightly different focus: "'I have the right to do anything,' you say—but not everything is beneficial. 'I have the right to do anything'—but not everything is constructive" (1 Corinthians 10:23).

In both cases, Paul contrasted a cultural emphasis on individual freedom (sound familiar?) with how those choices exercised in freedom impact us. Paul was essentially asking, *Is what you're choosing constructive? Is it beneficial? Is it mastering or enslaving you?*

Turning to the Old Testament, we find Solomon's wise counsel for every aspect of life: "Above all else, guard your heart, for everything you do flows from it" (Proverbs 4:23).

At the most foundational level, as we've seen throughout this book, entertainment influences our hearts. It stirs up emotion and has the power to shape our perspectives and worldviews with regard to what is right, true, and pure. (See Philippians 4:8 here for extra credit!) When we're deeply and emotionally engaged in a story, we may be influenced by the ideas or ideals it illustrates. And apart from intentional conversation and consideration afterward, we may not even realize that a well-told story has impacted—perhaps positively, perhaps not so positively—the way we see the world.

Now, one last passage to ponder. David wrote in Psalm 16:11, "You make known to me the path of life; *you will fill me* with joy in your presence, with eternal pleasures at your right hand" (emphasis added). Whether we realize it or not, God has designed us to be filled by a transcendent and intimate experience of His love. We long to be filled, so much so that we can't *not* seek it. And if that infilling isn't coming from God, we easily turn to our screens and to entertainment in search of a substitute and counterfeit experience of transcendence.

Blockbusters in their bombastic glory and their battles between good and evil give us a tiny taste of transcendence. But it's not the real thing. God has promised to fill us, but that filling may well involve practices that have become increasingly difficult in our culture of screens and entertainment: solitude and quietness before Him on one hand and gathering with the people of God to worship Him on the other.

When we combine the ideas seen in these passages of Scripture, we can establish a multilayered grid with questions to help ourselves and our children assess our media and entertainment choices:

- How might this choice influence me to embrace the world's values?
- Is this choice beneficial and constructive? Or am I being mastered by it?
- How is this affecting my heart?
- What am I choosing in an effort to fill myself?

Becoming Faithful Questioners

Dialogue may be the final approach of the three I've talked about in this chapter, but no matter where we are on that grid, we can model question asking for our kids and teach them to do it for themselves.

The ongoing conversation about entertainment can start with simple, age-appropriate questions after we've watched a movie or TV show together:

- What character did you like?
- Which character did you relate to the most and why?
- Was there anything that really encouraged you?
- Was there anything that disturbed you?

As our kids get older, our conversation can involve questions that go a bit deeper:

- What's the main message here?
- What is valued? What is criticized?
- How do those values compare and contrast with what we believe as Christians?

That last question especially has been great in launching conversations with my children. It also models critical thinking and teaches them that we don't have to be afraid of ideas or beliefs that differ from our own.

As our kids get used to these kinds of conversations, and as they mature and become able to engage in more sophisticated discussions, our questions naturally get deeper as we dig into more weighty, worldview-related issues:

- What questions does this piece of entertainment ask? What answers does it offer?
- How does this entertainment seek to influence us emotionally? How does it seek to persuade us rationally? Is it making arguments that appeal to the head or the heart? Or maybe both?
- What is the source of moral authority for values and decisions? Is it our individual experiences or feelings? A coherent belief system? God?
- What consequences do these characters experience for the choices they make? Do we see any negative repercussions for their beliefs or choices?

Leaving the Nest, Ready for the World

The goal with this dialogue approach to media and entertainment is that by the time our kids leave the nest, they'll be capable of recognizing how entertainment might be influencing them. We want to equip them to make choices that line up with biblical convictions that have been deeply internalized over the course of many years and many conversations.

We also want to give them plenty of opportunities to practice discernment regarding their entertainment choices. I mean that quite literally. Though there's no set age, at a certain point, it's time to give our kids the freedom to make their own entertainment choices, even if we don't always agree with them. By the time our children reach sixteen to eighteen years of age, we're acting not so much as *gatekeepers* but as *mentors*.

My son and I both love rock music, for instance. But I'm not always crazy about some of the bands he listens to. Instead of saying "Man, that's garbage. Turn it off!" my approach increasingly is more along the lines of having a Platonic discussion: "Hey, tell me about this band. What do you like about them? What do you relate to?"

We'll look at certain lyrics, and I'll ask him very specific questions about the beliefs and ideas and worldviews involved. More than once, in fact, I've asked my kids to write me a review of something they're watching or listening to. They roll their eyes and moan, "Daaaad!" But it's been fascinating to see what they have to say when they realize I'm dead serious about spurring them to think more deeply about the entertainment they choose—and the ideas therein.

Friends, it's a wild world out there when it comes to the ideas and ideals competing with the Christian faith for our kids' hearts and minds. That said, I'm convinced that when we focus on an ongoing relationship with our kids and engage them through dialogue, we can equip them to face the onslaught of worldviews and opinions with faith and a firm foundation.

Our goal isn't perfection. Rather, it's the commitment to keep engaging, keep talking, keep building relationship with them, always infused with truth and grace. And as they mature and begin to spread their wings, I believe we can have confidence that they have what it takes to soar.

PART 3

What to Pay Attention To

(and How)

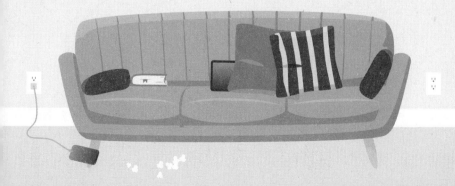

Screening Those Screens

Adam R. Holz

WE OFTEN TALK ABOUT SCREEN TIME as if it were a monolithic thing. As if watching a TV show and playing a video game impacted our brains in exactly the same way.

But the reality is, our pixelated windows offer vastly different views. Just as watching a show and playing a game offer us different experiences, they also impact us in different ways. So even though we use *screen time* as a shorthand descriptor for how we interact with this technology, we need to take another important step in understanding that how we *use* those screens is different—and provokes different potential issues.

Of course, when we look at entertainment as a whole, it

goes beyond those ever-present screens. We're dealing with books and music, too—two categories of entertainment that don't *require* screens at all (even if they often still make use of them).

Think of entertainment in terms of exercise. A rowing machine works on one part of your body; bench presses on another. Walking and running both work on your leg muscles, but they work entirely different muscles *in* those legs.

It's the same with entertainment, albeit not in such healthy ways. Books impact your mind and spirit in ways that television does not. Television scratches different itches in your brain and soul that games do not. It's all entertainment, but each category is as different from another as a jack-o'-lantern is from pumpkin pie.

Part of it has to do with the nature of the entertainment itself. Does it require us, say, to be active participants or passive consumers? Part of it involves how we *engage* with that entertainment. In other words, is it on a big or small screen? Do we consume it alone or with friends? And still another part has to do with how long, or how often, we're likely to engage with the entertainment too.

For example, let's say my favorite movie of all time is the original *Star Wars*. (Okay, it is. That's not a hypothetical at all.) I don't know how many times I've seen it. It's probably a big number. Maybe two hundred? Three hundred? Somewhere in the hundreds, I'm guessing.

That's a lot. But the vast majority of movies we'll likely see only once. The influence a movie has in that way is, then, relatively more limited compared to many—if not most—other forms of screen-based entertainment.

Bingeing a popular TV show might mean multiple seasons of ten or more episodes. What about social media? For many of us—and our kids—that's just part of the warp and woof of our days. Some folks might spend more than a movie's run time *every day* on Instagram or TikTok or whatever the newest thing is. With video games and their movie-like narratives, players can be engaged as *active*, rather than passive, participants in a storyline, along with the overall plot and its eventual outcome, for forty, fifty, or even *one hundred* hours or more.

As you can see, then, these forms of entertainment aren't the same at all. Which is why in this chapter we're going to take a look at them individually, giving you a brief overview of how these different categories work and how they might be influencing our kids when they engage with them. We'll look at movies and TV, video games and music, social media, YouTube, and newer, video-focused apps like TikTok.

MOVIES (PAUL ASAY)

"Cinema is the most beautiful fraud in the world."

So said Jean-Luc Godard, a highly regarded French-Swiss director whose movies I, and probably you, have never seen.[1] But while I don't know Godard's movies, I do like the quote. It gets at the contradiction at the heart of movies. They, perhaps more than any other form of screen-based entertainment we talk about in this chapter, are considered to be *art*.

They can certainly be beautiful. And most of them, on some level, lie.

Take *Avatar: The Way of Water*. James Cameron's block-buster takes us into the beautiful world of Pandora, a lush land that look so real you feel like you could go out and buy tickets to visit it. (And with Disney World's newish Pandora-themed playground, I suppose you can.) Several secular reviewers called it a masterpiece. Another called it "pure cinematic visual magic."[2]

And, naturally, it manipulates you at every turn.

Flickering Influences

I don't mean that in a *bad* way necessarily (though if you don't like *Avatar*'s environmental message, you certainly might see it that way). As mentioned earlier, pretty much every movie is designed to manipulate you. The score swells at certain junctures to make you feel touched and inspired. The cinematography is structured to give you a certain vibe. *All* stories do this: the ones you read, the ones you play, the ones you listen to. But *movies*, because of their budgets and run time and the fact that most are designed to be beamed onto screens a couple of stories tall, are particularly effective.

Cameron's *The Way of Water*[3] is a simple story, but its very simplicity helps illustrate the manipulation that Cameron, as a storyteller, engages in.

In the movie's first hour, the director gives us a beautiful, unspoiled, and wholly imaginary world to gasp over. He takes his time showing Pandora's watery beauty. He introduces us to sentient, whale-like creatures that form critical bonds with the local "people." The people themselves—the blue-skinned Na'vi—are tall, lithe, unwrinkled, and unblemished.

In the second act, we see the movie's colonizing, pillaging enemies: us. While not *every* human is bad, we as a species seemed determined to burn, mine, and apparently pave beautiful Pandora, turning it into a wasteland that resembles Mordor (another bit of storytelling manipulation). Humans look short and clumsy compared with the statuesque Na'vi, and our attitudes match: We're clearly eager to subdue, not savor, this wonderland. We watch a particularly vile set of humans slaughter a whale-like creature—one that we've met before—for just a gallon or two of an antiaging elixir. The rest of the beast's carcass is left to rot, and its orphaned calf is left to die.

The final hour of the movie pits Cameron's good versus evil, putting the climax of the film on the burning, sinking wreckage of a whaling vessel. Visually the message is clear: Humankind might destroy this beautiful world and themselves along with it—just as Cameron believes we're doing with our very real one.

"We do a lot of things as the human species that are really deleterious to . . . fragile ecosystems," Cameron told CNET. "A lot of the animals we're seeing and enjoying and learning from in our series are at risk. They're under threat. And by the way, the human species is at risk and under threat. Potentially even an existential threat if you go out far enough, a couple hundred years or so. Maybe even sooner."[4]

It's no small feat to turn a movie audience—pretty much all of whom would qualify as human, after all—to root against its own kind and turn us, as a species, into monsters. And indeed, Cameron might've had a harder time had he taken *The Way of Water* straight to TV. Cameron's environmental message wouldn't be nearly as impactful if it wasn't delivered on a giant screen. Watch the thing in 3D, and the experience becomes even bigger and more visceral. The greens and blues of Pandora are lush and vivid. The explosions and fires caused by us humans are all the more dastardly and devastating.

We're Going to Need a Bigger Screen

While the world of moviemaking is changing, and while movies are arguably losing that top spot in the entertainment hierarchy, they still tell their stories in unique and, on some level, unmatched ways. There's still something special about going to a movie. And that makes them especially influential.

Think about how different it is to go to a movie theater versus watching something on TV. For the movies, you have to, you know, *get dressed*. No pj's and bathrobes for you. You make plans. You plop down your money and set aside two hours or more to just sit and *receive* something. Movies are not just a mere diversion—something to do when we have some time to kill. They are, more often than not, *events*. For a *big* movie—the newest *Star Wars* flick or superhero saga—we and/or our kids might've been looking forward to it for *months*.

And because of the planning, intentionality, and anticipation that going to the movies entails, we're primed to receive whatever the film aims to deliver.

When you add people to the mix? It becomes all the more powerful.

There's a reason we sometimes get goose bumps when we sing in church, beyond the beauty of the music and the power of the moment. It's all the people singing with us. When we're at a sporting event, we stand up and cheer until our voices are hoarse. Few of us do this sort of thing when we're alone. There's an energy that comes from experiencing something with other people.

For many of us, most forms of entertainment can be ingested alone. We read books alone. We listen to music on our isolating earbuds. We watch YouTube on tiny, solitary screens. When we do share that stuff with others, though, it ramps up the entertainment a notch. It's not just good enough to watch or listen to. It's good enough to share.

Movies are *meant* to be shared. More often than not, you're going with friends or family. Even if you go alone, you're surrounded by people, and you're all engaged in the same thing. It's a communal experience, and that comes with its own power. Have you noticed how *good* movies generate their own sort of energy in the confines of a theater? How the laughing audience makes a comedy's jokes funnier? How the creepy vibe of a horror movie is all the creepier? How, when the hero saves the day and the audience claps, you're more likely to clap along? Even though *no one involved in the movie can hear you*?

Perhaps for those reasons—the event-like aura they take on, the communal energy they generate, the funnier humor and the creepier horror—and all sorts of others, movies, more than anything else we discuss here, can be treated with near-sacred reverence. And perhaps that's also why Christian storytellers often tell their stories on the biggest screen they can. They know the power of the medium. They know the sway movies can have, because they've felt it themselves.

But if the message of a movie is a *bad* one, that can make it all the more damaging. Sex scenes can be all the more salacious. Violence can be all the more cringeworthy. F-words at the decibels we hear in movie theaters feel as though they're literally pounding in your ear. And the movie's messages? Its morals? If those run counter to biblical truth, they can be all the harder to see in the moment and dispel in the aftermath.

Changing Cinema

In an age where many movies are going straight to streaming services, some of the traditional majesty of this genre of entertainment—its magic, if you will—is lost. What we gain in quick access to bathrooms and snacks, we lose in the storytelling oomph, the ancillary elements that help make movies what Godard called that "beautiful fraud." For families, that's paradoxically a bit of good news. It's easier now to pause a movie and talk through its issues. It's *far* easier to turn it off and walk away if it crosses the line.

And yet, the shimmer and glimmer of the movies remains. Some of a movie's charm—and by that I mean its ability to capture our imagination in good ways and bad—still glows. In this era, where a two-minute YouTube video seems like an eternity, a two-hour movie is still an event. You still settle in to watch it, more than likely, with intent and anticipation. Even in an age filled with so many screens, in a world that offers us so many distractions, movies still beckon. They bring us in virtually and ask us to sit for a spell. And the spell they cast can be as powerful as it ever was.

We've talked about how best to navigate the world of movies in previous chapters. But as a reminder, parents need to take a few special steps to keep their kids' movie viewing in check.

1. **Be aware.** Don't let your children go to movies that don't have your approval. (Obviously, the younger they are, the more important this is.) Know what sorts of flicks might be on tap during sleepovers. Watch films with your kids when you can. And, of course, always try to research what might be in a movie before giving your okay. (We, naturally, think *Plugged In* is the best place for this sort of thing, but other resources can be helpful too.)

2. **Be alert.** As we saw in the previous chapter, as parents we need to be mindful of how our children might react to certain elements in the movies they watch. If possible, watch *with* them and tune in to their reactions. Feel free to skip over certain scenes. Pause the movie and talk through any problem points.

3. **Be available.** When I watch a movie, I sometimes don't know what I think about it until the day after, when I start writing the review. I'm not immune to

a movie's manipulation, and sometimes I can be so swept up in the music and the story and the emotional climax that it's not till the next morning that I think, *Hey, that movie didn't make a lick of sense.*

I think we can all react differently to movies, given an opportunity to think and reflect. You can encourage reflection by talking with your kids about a movie afterward and asking some of the questions we suggested earlier in this book or by asking some of your own. And if your kids have their own questions—whether the day or the week or the month after—be available to talk with them. Remember, the beauty and power of movies is, in part, how communal they can be. All the more important to let your children know that you're working through this particular movie together.

TELEVISION (PAUL ASAY)

For decades now, movies have been entertainment's unquestioned crème de la crème of storytelling mediums. Television, meanwhile, was its tagalong little sister. The top directors plied their craft on the silver screen. With some exceptions, the world's top actors would spend their careers in movies—only stooping to do a television show if their careers were on the decline and they had a yacht payment to make. Big stories demanded a big screen, the thinking went. Television had to content itself with *Gilligan's Island* and *Dynasty*.

No more.

The biggest, buzziest stories these days are serialized.

While the world of cinema shoots out its sequels and super-hero movies, TV gives us creative, complex, and ridiculously addictive shows that spur watercooler conversations nationwide.

Consider the fourth season of Netflix's *Stranger Things*, which racked up more than one billion hours of total view time in just five days.[5] The nostalgia-driven sci-fi show became the very definition of must-see TV. Because Netflix releases most of its seasons all at once, about 361,000 people binge-watched season 2 of *Stranger Things* within *twenty-four hours* of its launch.[6] (No mean feat, given that the nine-episode season ran for thirteen hours.) Or think of AMC's *Breaking Bad*, a wildly problematic morality fable that took some time to get traction but, by its final season, had more than ten million viewers—huge numbers in this fractured entertainment age of ours.[7]

But in terms of buzz, ratings, and influence, most everything may take a back seat to HBO's *Game of Thrones*.

For eight seasons between 2011 and 2019, *Thrones* (based on a series of books by George R. R. Martin) dominated the cultural conversation. Despite being on a premium platform that a lot of people didn't even have, the fantasy epic racked up viewership stats thought to be impossible these days. During its last season, the average episode drew an estimated forty-six million viewers.[8] That's more than *twice* the number of people who watched NBC's *Sunday Night Football*.[9] It's also still television's most pirated show, with pirated episodes "accounting for around 230 *billion* views a year."[10]

Winter Isn't Coming: It's Here

Game of Thrones also neatly illustrates the particular pitfalls of television. In decades past, most TV shows were filtered through the Federal Communications Commission (FCC) and had to meet some basic broadcast standards: no sex or nudity, no extreme violence, only mild swear words. While those standards are still in play (in some respects) for broadcast networks (ABC, CBS, NBC, Fox, and the CW), it's the Wild West everywhere else. And *Thrones* was as wild as they came.

As Kennedy Unthank noted earlier in the book, *Thrones* wasn't just a compelling show. Some of its most avid viewers treated it as pornography. Most of its episodes (particularly in its first several seasons) featured graphic, gratuitous sex and nudity—so much so that it introduced the word *sexposition* into the cultural conversation. (Writer Myles McNutt created the term during its first season, noting the show's tendency to allow the characters to talk about critical plot points while engaged in intimacies.)[11] The violence was equally ridiculous. And the language? Well, let's just say the f-word found a friendly home in the fictional world of Westeros.

Game of Thrones was hardly the first show to include graphic content. But its success told storytellers that they could be both wildly problematic *and* popular. Nearly all television shows deemed to be "must-watch" today are rated TV-MA—the equivalent of an R-rating or worse. And some shows are absolutely worse.

That's right: The biggest shows on TV often would make their R-rated movie counterparts blush. But some would-be viewers and their families are still operating under the assumption that TV shows tend to be *less* problematic. The fact that television's most salacious series also tend to draw the most buzz compounds the problem: A show's popularity may lure some into thinking that it can't be *that bad* if so many people—including their own friends—are watching it. Not only might that lure more faith-minded viewers (including teens and even kids) to consider watching deeply problematic shows, but it also encourages them to minimize the show's issues. Series such as *Game of Thrones* have effectively lowered the bar for everyone else: What was considered almost unthinkable for airing on TV a decade or two ago is now very much the norm.

Those problems are compounded, exponentially, by the time we spend with a given binge. Consider: *Game of Thrones* has a total run time of more than seventy hours. That's more than six times what it would take for you to watch the extended version of Peter Jackson's *Lord of the Rings* trilogy and about thirty-five times that of an average movie. That kind of long-term exposure makes for a more enriching, engrossing, and—this is key—*influential* entertainment experience. While few *Game of Thrones* viewers will start beheading their neighbors, seventy hours of "sexposition" and f-words are hard to watch without some impact to the viewer's heart, mind, and spirit.

What to Do with the Small Screen's Big Problems

Given the proliferation of screens in most homes—not just multiple TVs but also phones and laptops and tablets as well—trying to tame this stampede of unsavory television shows can seem almost hopeless. But believe it or not, you do have some tools at your fingertips.

Dam the Streams

Be mindful of the sorts of streaming services you subscribe to. No, let's go further: Be *ruthless*. No one's forcing you to cough up monthly cash for Netflix or Disney+. While most popular streaming services have stuff that's suitable and fun for the whole family, those quality shows mingle with series that might make a Lannister from *Game of Thrones* blush. The most reliable way to keep those problematic shows from reaching your child's or teen's eyes is by simply keeping the given streaming service from flowing into your home.

Oh, and when you stop shoveling your money into some of those more problematic services, it might help send a message to them too. You—and loads of viewers like you—want good, quality, compelling programs without the filth. Many storytellers seem to think that to tell a good story you need a generous amount of sex, swear words, and violence. That's not the case, and perhaps they could use a little encouragement to see that.

Use Parental Controls

If you can't do without a streaming service, learn how to set some parental guidelines on that service. Most, if not all, major streamers come with parental control options. Most parents simply ignore them, leaving their young sons and daughters to flip on something wholly inappropriate when Mom and Dad are out of the room.

Plugged In offers video tutorials on how to navigate the parental controls on most big streaming services. We'll take you through the process of setting it up and managing it, step by step. But you should be aware of two potential pitfalls of parental controls.

First, while such controls can help filter out shows with the most obvious problematic content—sex, language, smoking, and so on—they will not help you at all in screening out shows with prickly worldview issues. Take Netflix's *She-Ra and the Princesses of Power*, for instance. The animated kids' series is one of the most LGBT-friendly shows around. "On Etheria, princesses are just as likely to be married to each other as they are to have boyfriends," notes Tracy Brown of the *Los Angeles Times*.[12] "Not even the most ruthless villain around has trouble remembering anybody's pronouns. It's a planet where gender isn't constricted, heteronormativity does not exist, and queer people just get to be." And *She-Ra* is rated TV-Y7, which means that it would skate through all but the most restrictive of Netflix's parental control filters.

Second, here's something you already know: Kids are smart, and a particularly determined child or teen can likely find ways to circumvent any safeguards you set in place.

Consider Christian Alternatives

One of the most exciting developments in the world of television has been the explosion of Christian and family friendly streaming services. Pure Flix features scads of original programs and movies. Minno brands itself as the "#1 source of Christian content for kids," and it includes the eternally popular *VeggieTales* series. Great American Family offers original programming and some classic, family friendly shows from yesteryear.

And, of course, all the tips I've shared with you in the movies section of this chapter are as important as ever: Be aware, be alert, be available. Know what your kids are watching, and familiarize yourself with the shows they like. (*Plugged In* has thousands of TV reviews to help you.) Watch shows with your kids whenever possible, and always be available to answer questions or talk over concerns. Dialoguing with your children is the single best weapon you have in the realm of television consumption.

MUSIC (ADAM HOLZ)

In some significant ways, popular music might just be the biggest outlier among the entertainment mediums we're talking about in this chapter. For one thing—and you may have thought about this already—it's an *auditory* medium, not a visual one.

Technically, you don't need a screen to enjoy it. In fact, the last decade or so has seen a huge resurgence in vinyl record sales—in part a reaction against the way digital music compresses sound and robs it of its quality. My teenage son, for example, has gotten on the vinyl bandwagon, and he's always looking for old records to add to his growing collection.

Having said that, the vast majority of people listening to music today aren't listening to some physical medium—a vinyl record, a CD, or a (wait for it) cassette tape (for those old enough to have purchased such a thing). No, music today is predominantly a digitally distributed medium. With music-based apps such as Spotify, Pandora, Apple Music, and YouTube, among others, most of the popular music recorded in the past hundred years is probably streaming somewhere. Much of the time, it's available for free, but in some cases, a subscription service is needed to locate more obscure or exclusive stuff.

Music still comes with a video component for many consumers. Some of the most popular videos can each garner upward of one billion views on YouTube.

So what do we need to know about music? And what do we need to consider regarding the unique way music influences young (and perhaps not-so-young) listeners and fans?

Music's Influence

Of all the forms of entertainment we discuss in this book, I would argue that music remains potentially the most influential, for primarily two overlapping reasons: First, the music we love tends to resonate with us in profoundly personal ways; and second, we listen to it over and over (and over and over). That combination of personal connection and repetition can create a potent recipe for tweens or teens to get lost in their favorite band's songs . . . and to be influenced and shaped by that music.

At the risk of sounding like I'm eight thousand years old, let me share a personal story here. When I was growing up in the eighties, music was my refuge. I put headphones on and rewound my cassettes until they wore out. My *music*—not movies, not TV, not video games—was the emotional balm that anesthetized my adolescence. Perhaps you had a similar experience.

I gravitated toward metal and rock. I can still viscerally

remember singing Whitesnake's hit "Here I Go Again," something I identified with at a deep level.

The lyrics of the chorus tell the story of a drifter, living life and walking down roads all on his own.[13] The song reinforced my already-deep sense that I was alone, that I was on my own, and that it would always be that way. At sixteen, having an anthem that enabled me to articulate so fiercely my sense of alienation seemed like a gift.

As an adult looking back, I can recognize that the song distorted my sense of identity in ways that likely reinforced the sense of isolation I felt so deeply. (Virtually all teens feel isolated at some point, of course, but that's another conversation for another time.)

Music's influence comes from how we identify personally with lyrics that express our innermost hurts and insecurities and fears and longings. For kids who process their emotions through music, that connection is reinforced almost perpetually as they listen to their favorite songs and artists.

In the introduction to this chapter, I noted that I may well have seen the original *Star Wars* several hundred times. There are scenes and moments I love, images that still give me goose bumps. (The twin suns setting on Tatooine as Luke looks wistfully at the horizon, for example, is my favorite movie scene of all time.) But as powerful as our favorite movie scenes may be, I'd argue that they pale in comparison to the emotional connection forged between an artist and a fan. One of my favorite songs of all time is Bon Jovi's "Livin' on a Prayer." If I've seen *Star Wars* a couple hundred times,

I might have listened to that song three hundred times in a *week* when it was released in 1986. Total lifetime tally on that one? I wouldn't be a bit surprised if it's ten thousand listens or more—every one an emotion-drenched, four-minute dopamine hit that still gives me a feel-good thrill nearly forty years later.

Not every kid is wired to connect so deeply and emotionally with music. But for those who are? I don't think any other entertainment medium touches popular music for the overall time spent with it and the potential for its messages about life, death, love, sex, meaning, and purpose (or lack thereof) to shape a young person's heart and soul.

One other scientific finding worth noting: Have you ever wondered why the music of your youth is so much more powerful than most of what you hear after you're out of your teen years? Yes, the volatility of adolescence is certainly in play. But there's even more going on here than you might have realized. Scientists have discovered that because a young person's brain is still forming during this season, one biological consequence of this process is the way our brains bond with our favorite music. In 2014, *Slate* music critic Mark Joseph Stern reported on this phenomenon:

> Why do the songs I heard when I was teenager sound sweeter than anything I listen to as an adult? . . . In recent years, psychologists and neuroscientists have confirmed that these songs hold disproportionate power over our emotions. And researchers have

uncovered evidence that suggests our brains bind us to the music we heard as teenagers more tightly than anything we'll hear as adults—a connection that doesn't weaken as we age. Musical nostalgia, in other words, isn't just a cultural phenomenon: It's a neuronic command. And no matter how sophisticated our tastes might otherwise grow to be, our brains may stay jammed on those songs we obsessed over during the high drama of adolescence.[14]

Identifying with Musicians

More than other forms of entertainment, I'd also argue that music fans identify with their favorite artists on a deeply personal level. After working at *Plugged In* for more than twenty years, I've found that some of the angriest emails we get are from teens who are offended that we would call into question a given artist's outlook on life. More than once, reviews I've written for *Plugged In* end up being quoted on fan message boards—usually not in a good way—if fans thought I misunderstood or misrepresented an artist's message or meaning. There simply is no fury like that of an offended music fan.

As we think about music's influence, then, we need to realize that a beloved artist's influence extends beyond the songs themselves to the artist's personal life as well. Many musicians over the years have tried to downplay the idea that they are role models. But there's simply no denying that for tweens or teens, identifying with their favorite singers also creates a deep sympathy for their viewpoints, perspectives, and worldviews.

Today's Music Content

It's axiomatic when it comes to music (and perhaps pop culture in general) that we tend to look back on yesteryear and elevate the content of our own era over anything being produced today. It's also pretty common to believe that what's happening today is worse, content-wise, than anything from yesteryear.

Still, there's more than a little bit of truth to the perception that popular music today continues to push into more explicit territory, lyrically speaking, than much of what we'd find in previous decades.

In the most popular genres of rap and R & B, sexually explicit content—including in songs that chart well and are played on mainstream radio stations—is often borderline pornographic. In 2020, for example, Cardi B and Megan Thee Stallion hit the top of the charts with the hit "WAP," a crude anatomical acronym. The lyrics were even more anatomically graphic than the title. Far from being denounced as pornographic, many commentators praised Cardi B for her "sex-positive" stance.

We can find myriad other examples to illustrate the state of things in music these days. But the most important thing we can do as parents is to, first, be aware of what our kids and teens are listening to and, second, enter into the conversation about the choices our kids are making.

Those conversations don't necessarily have to be completely negative and cautionary, either. They can open up opportunities to talk with our children honestly about topics that might be hard to tackle otherwise. After all, perhaps more than any other entertainment medium, song lyrics offer a ready-made chance to talk with our kids about worldviews and beliefs. We can listen to a song together and ask some basic questions:

- What does this song praise? Condemn?
- What does the song or artist say the "good life" consists of?
- How does the content of this song—what the artist is saying—line up with what we believe as followers of Jesus?
- If someone behaved the way we hear in this song, what do you think would happen?

Unlike a movie, which requires a couple of hours of time investment, a popular song can serve as a bridge to a broader conversation about worldview and values in just a couple of minutes. Lyrics to virtually any song you can think of are easily available online to facilitate this conversation.

BOOKS (PAUL ASAY)

When I was about ten years old, I picked up *The Last Battle*, C. S. Lewis's climactic book in his Chronicles of Narnia series. In the book, there's a scene wherein it seems as though the tide of that final battle is about to turn. Talking horses are let loose and race to enter the fray. But before they reach the fight, some agnostic dwarves point their bows at the horses, loose their arrows, and shoot them down. Every last one.[15]

It's the first time I ever cried while engaging in a bit of

entertainment. Even today, writing those words makes me achingly sad.

If music was Adam's particular jam growing up, books were mine. By the time I could read, I was hooked: My mom enjoyed reading aloud to me, but she never could finish a book; so when she stopped reading, I'd pick it up and read the rest. While I've watched my share of movies and TV shows, played plenty of video games, and listened to loads of music, nothing in my life has influenced me more than good, old-fashioned books. I think most avid readers—many of whom are kids—would agree with me.

Page-Turners

At first blush, it seems strange to think of books as so influential. They don't jam your mind with lewd images or startle you with jump scares. They don't have the benefit of snarling guitars or soaring scores to drive their points home. They are as simple and straightforward as a bit of entertainment can be: black print on white pages. Yet, for all the technological advancements we've made in entertaining ourselves, books can still change our outlooks, our worldviews, our very lives in ways unmatched by other forms of entertainment. The Bible—the most beautiful, contextual, and powerful book there is—is proof of that.

But why do books resonate so deeply with those who read them? I think it comes down to two simple reasons. The first is *posture*. No, not whether you're slouching when you read. I'm talking about mental posture. Books force us to actively engage—to metaphorically lean forward. Most other forms of entertainment tend to be passive. We literally sit back and watch a story unfold before us. It requires nothing of us other than our attention.

Books (and the other big exception, games) require us to be active participants in the story. The process of ingesting paragraph after paragraph requires another level of attention from the reader. We engage on the sort of level we would when we're having a deep conversation with a friend—not passively absorbing as we would a lecture or sermon. And inherently, because we're leaning forward, in a sense, that makes us more active participants in the story being told. Even though it's just words on a page, it becomes more real, more tangible, more alive.

And that brings us to the second simple reason why books resonate with avid readers: *imagination*. I believe that those of us who love to read also tend to have powerful imaginations—the ability to conjure vivid images of what's being described in a book and to, in a sense, root ourselves more deeply in the book's narrative. We're not just watching Frodo and the Fellowship of the Nine struggle up snowy Caradhras in Tolkien's *Fellowship of the Ring*; we're shivering beside them. We're not just reading about World War I in *All Quiet on the Western Front*. We can feel the horror ourselves. And while both of those works have been translated quite effectively into movies, the books feel more real to me. Why? Because the images I created in reading them are, literally, a part of me—my own creations, my own addendums to the stories.

That's a critical point. Because we become a part of these

books and the books, in a way, become part of us, we're far more susceptible to their influence.

All Quiet on the Western Front (which unspools the final days of World War I from the point of view of a German soldier) is a good example for me. I read Erich Maria Remarque's book when I was about seventeen—an age when my faith was still in formation and I was about the same age as the book's narrator. Remarque's brutal, horrific depiction of life on the front impacted me deeply. But deeper still was a sense of the meaninglessness of it all and the finality of death.

"While [our commanders] continued to write and talk, we saw the wounded and dying," Remarque wrote. "While they taught that duty to one's country is the greatest thing, we already knew that death-throes are stronger."[16]

How could a loving and just God allow such things? I thought as I read. I was taught to believe (and still believe) that God is the greatest storyteller of all, and that as such, every word He writes in our lives has meaning and purpose. The world that unfolded in *All Quiet on the Western Front* deeply shook my sense of certainty. It took some time for me to reconcile Remarque's terrible tale with the truths of Scripture. I had to relearn, in essence, that the Bible itself tells us how "meaningless" life can be: Ecclesiastes presents us with that side of existence in poetical, painful detail.

Remarque was telling his readers a grave truth. But even truth, when not the whole truth, can mislead impressionable readers. And when a story is false, it can be all the more damaging.

Judge a Book Not by Its Cover but by Its Content

If you have avid readers in your family, first, congratulations! I think that's great. But they could still use your help choosing great books over bad ones and learning how to separate a book's metaphorical wheat from its chaff. This comes down to a few elements we outlined earlier.

Be Aware

It's not nearly as easy to guard the entertainment gate in terms of books, because books can come from a dizzying number of sources—the school library, friends, family members, even from under the Christmas tree. And because we tend to think that books are good ("At least she's reading, right?"), we might be inclined to let our normal discernment disciplines slide. Given how influential books are, that'd be a mistake. Monitor the books your kids want to read as much as you can, telling them no if you feel that something's off-limits. Lean on our *Plugged In* book reviews whenever possible. If we haven't covered something (it's impossible to review every book, given the number of them out there), consider reading it yourself. And that relates to the next point.

Be Engaged

This, you'll note, is different from the "alert" tag mentioned in movies. Again, this gets to the unique nature of books. While books can indeed be incredibly influential in a reader's life—particularly if that reader is young—readers are automatically more engaged with books' stories too. Because they're taking a more active role, they're innately thinking about the characters and concepts. They're often considering what they'd do in a given character's place or how their own lives or feelings look similar to the character's. They may even be weighing the book's messages—even if they're not aware they're doing so. In other words, they're thinking about what they're consuming, and that's a huge part of what we'd encourage any media and entertainment consumer to do.

That active posture makes books, *generally speaking*, slightly more navigable than movies or television shows in a way. But it also requires that you, as a parent, engage too.

If you land on a book that you feel is navigable for your children, consider reading it to them. Or with them. Or alongside them. This gives you the opportunity to form a little book club with them so you can talk through any problem points or discuss any problematic characters. It can help you stress a book's good points. And, most importantly, it can help you connect with your young reader in a deeply personal way. If a book's important to your son or daughter, and it becomes important to you, that's something you can share long after you put it back on the shelf.

I'm reminded of my poor mother, who never had a chance to finish a book. Even so, I can still hear her voice reading books to me. I could feel the enjoyment as she read. And the fact that we could enjoy those precious moments together was *priceless*.

Be Available

Whether you read together or not, be there to help your kids through the inevitable questions that books can stir up. Ask your own questions about the book you're reading. What do you like about it? Which character most resonates with you? Do you think you would make the same choice she did? When something's important to any of us, we want to talk about it with someone, and books can feel incredibly important. Be a sounding board for your children. You don't have to teach them any lessons through the book (though you can). You don't have to critique the book (though sometimes you should). First, *listen*—thoughtfully and carefully. Then engage. Talk with them at their level. Try to understand their joy or pain or confusion. Be there.

GAMES (BOB HOOSE)

Not all that long ago, if you asked some friends to play a video game with you, they would instantly think of a little room packed with large, stand-alone arcade consoles and maybe an air hockey table or a few pinball machines. Those places were called *arcade rooms* and were generally the *only* way to play a video game way back in the 1970s. The games were fun, diversionary distractions that would quickly suck up a young person's allowance or empty a shelf-dwelling piggy bank. And back in the day, platform games such as *Asteroids*, *Space Invaders*, and *PAC-MAN* were pretty much the only thing everyone wanted to save their quarters for.

Today, however, arcade games like that are so rare that if you stumble upon one, it's akin to stepping into a museum piece snatched out of time. And if the average teen *does* see an arcade game, they'll likely just smirk before going back to their phone. Because these days you can play games by the score on nearly any screen you encounter—powered by everything from high-tech game consoles and computers to that ubiquitous little device in your back pocket. In fact, compared to the tech powering your phone, those older gaming iterations are the equivalent of banging two rocks together.

Let's not forget the available genres in today's catalog (*PAC-MAN*, pshaw!). These days, you can find strategy games, shooters, fighting games, casual party games, simulations, role-playing games, action-adventure titles, sports games, combat games—and the list goes on and on. We do indeed live in a *very* large world of gaming.

But is that a good thing or a problem? Are games easing our day-to-day stresses or adding to them? Are they making us better or worse? And how do you navigate your family's experience with those amusements?

The *g* in *game* stands for . . . good?

You may well be a longtime naysayer when it comes to the topic of video games, but the fact is that as researchers have looked closely at gaming, they've come away with quite a few positives.

For instance, studies have shown that games can boost our cognitive abilities, especially in the key areas of concentration and something called *visuospatial skills*. Our visuospatial abilities control how our brains remember objects and the spatial relations between those objects. We use these skills when we're driving a car and reading a map, for instance. And these skills can even help students when it comes to visualizing math and engineering problems.

Improved hand-eye coordination between what's seen

on-screen and what's done with a controller in your hand is a big plus too. Those improved abilities can help with real-world activities such as riding a bike, typing, juggling, playing tennis, and other tasks that require coordination between your hands and your eyes.

Studies have also shown that games—with all their challenges and obstacles—can be very helpful in improving a gamer's problem-solving skills and logic. They can even have positive physical effects on our brains. MRI scans have shown that gamers develop more gray matter after playing through gaming challenges over time. Why is that important? Well, gray-matter tissue creates more brain connections and can affect our decision making, for one thing. Kids and adults who play video games regularly make faster, more accurate decisions than their nongaming peers. In turn, that also boosts a player's self-confidence when they begin to attain in-game successes.

Games have been associated with better memory and lower stress levels too.

Bad games, bad!

So am I saying that video games are the solution to all your problems and that you can stop worrying about any of those red flags you may have seen about gaming in the past?

Nope.

Games come with significant problems, too. Some studies have associated gaming with sleep deprivation, insomnia, depression, and anxiety. Oh, and then there's that dopamine release I mentioned. As we learned in chapter 2, we can get hooked on those pleasure zaps to our brains.

Experts are even worried about "internet gaming disorder," which the World Health Organization (WHO) has classified as a gaming addiction that can involve becoming preoccupied with games, feeling lousy when we can't play, losing interest in other activities, and even abandoning relationships or career opportunities because we can't put down that controller.[17]

And on another brain front, a recent brain-imaging study published in the journal *Psychology of Popular Media* showed credible evidence that heavily *violent* video game consumption can lead to a desensitization to painful images and a reduced empathy for other people's pain.[18]

So which is it then?

If you're currently frowning and grumbling that I should make up my mind—*Are games good or bad?*—I don't blame you. But the fact is, the studies have seemingly come down on both sides of the same equation. However, if you look closely enough, that's really not the case at all.

Navigating Game Use

The fact is that gaming is really no different from any other media we consume on a regular basis. If someone is constantly watching slasher movies or endlessly streaming foul-mouthed comedies or nasty rap albums, it's *all* going to have a negative effect. The same holds true with games . . . only maybe even more so for two reasons: first, because of how long you can spend playing some games, and second, because of how your brain is immersed in those games. When we actively engage in a game—instead of being more passive, as we might be when watching movies or television shows—our brains are just more involved in the action. For this reason, games are expert teaching tools (in good ways and bad) and significant mood influencers. And when you think about the fifty-plus hours that gamers can spend playing a given game, that's a lot of influence.

I mentioned earlier that some studies have linked games to sleep deprivation, insomnia, depression, anxiety, and addiction. Do you see any common threads there? Spending too much time gaming is one of them. As with any other activities that have potential benefits and harms, moderation is key. The kinds of games your kids are playing is another element connected to gaming downsides. If they're immersed in dark, violent, foul games, it only makes sense that they could find themselves desensitized, depressed, and anxious.

As parents, we can limit or eliminate the potential harms of gaming by curbing the number of hours our families spend playing them (individually or together); becoming more discerning about the games we play; and knowing when to turn off the screen, get some exercise, and—I don't know—maybe socialize in the real world with real people for a while.

So with that in mind, let's explore some helpful guidelines that you can adapt for your family.

Establish Time Limits

There is absolutely no reason parents and kids can't all sit down and set some decent limits on how long is too long and how long is just right for gaming. It's probably going to be different for different families and individuals, but one rule of thumb is that the younger the kid, the less time should be spent playing video games. The American Academy of Pediatrics recommends that parents limit gaming for school-age kids to no more than sixty minutes per day on school days and two hours or less on other days.[19] For children under the age of six, the group recommends no more than one hour per day. You can modify these guidelines for your family . . . and then stick to them.

Bedrooms Are Gadget-Free

You've probably heard this a dozen times already, but phones, consoles, and screens should be kept out of the bedroom. Period. Screens of any sort have a siren's call at night when the brain is begging for just a few minutes more of entertainment. Besides, if you can keep game consoles and the like in shared areas of your home, it's easier for *everyone* to see what's being played on them. (Dark, foul, bloody games just love a darkened bedroom with the door shut.)

Go Multiplayer, Young Man

If your family has a gaming console, look into games you can play together. There are gazillions of fun games (sports games, adventure games, Pokémon games, etc.) that you can play with your kids on your phones or in a local co-op with a couple of controllers. These amusements are generally light and fun and can be played in relatively short stretches.

And You Play Too

Mom and/or Dad should get into the gaming action as well. Here's a little secret: When you play games with your kids, you'll have one more thing in common when the teen years roll around (those barren days when teens and parents tend to exist in different orbits and angrily frown at one another). If you enjoy playing games together, it can help lower the parent-child wall that can start piling up between you. While you're gaming together, it's easier to slip into casual conversations about the things of life. Secret number two: Being a gamer also allows you to point out potential gaming issues when you see them and help your kids on the discernment side of choosing the games they play.

Don't Demand; Just Talk It Out

Let's face it, when kids are tiny, it's easy to control everything they play or say no to whatever you don't like or think might be harmful. But those kingly and queenly rulings get harder with every passing year. So start conversations and connections early on. Keep your eyes and ears open about the changing state of games and gaming, and spend time as a family discussing the pros and cons. Oh, and don't hesitate to check out PluggedIn.com for helpful reviews and pointers.

YOUTUBE (KENNEDY UNTHANK)

Sometimes our brains store utterly unimportant childhood moments in our long-term memory, causing us to wonder, *Why do I even remember that?* Well, one of mine involves the first time I heard about YouTube.

It was 2008, and I was in third grade. As my classmates and I were leaving gym class, a friend of mine told me that there was a video on YouTube I just *had* to see: a FilmCow video titled "Charlie the Unicorn," wherein a couple of multicolored unicorns harass their cynical friend to visit the mythical Candy Mountain.[20] (Prospective viewers should note that the video and the series that followed involve a bit of violence, swearing, and nonsensical humor.)

I went home that day and watched the video. And before I knew it, a flood of other early viral videos and channels began to take up my time. Videos like "Charlie Bit My Finger," "David after Dentist," and "Double Rainbow" provided our family with a steady supply of quotes for years to come.

As the video-sharing website began to grow in popularity, so, too, did its first stars. Names of YouTubers and channels began to circulate as commonly as celebrity icons did: Fred, Smosh, PewDiePie, nigahiga, Jenna Marbles, Annoying Orange. YouTube added the ability to "like" and comment on videos, incentivizing more people to visit the website. As the site experimented with advertisements, top creators were paid in ad revenue for bringing in views and clicks, causing others to start creating content too. Some creators even began getting paid enough to justify working as YouTubers *full-time*, making videos more frequently and enhancing quality. YouTubers with more views were even able to gain sponsorships, justify selling personalized merchandise, and hire teams to edit and manage their content.

All this growth set the stage for YouTube's domination of social media. As the site's selection of content grew, more and more users found videos that appealed to them. And as the number of creators increased, people were more likely to find YouTubers they enjoyed watching.

Those two factors—the selection of content and the charisma of creators—made YouTube a momentous force in both the entertainment and the social media industries. (We'll talk about those factors in more detail in the next section.) Because of the large variety of videos and creators, YouTube allows its users to not only find the exact niche that tickles their fancy but also the charismatic video creators who focus on making those niche videos. On YouTube, users can search for content as niche as "marble run" or "garage sale pickers" and find dozens of channels that exist entirely to make videos about those topics. Few other streaming services can compete with that level of specificity.

YouTube isn't going anywhere. In fact, by many measures, it's the most important entertainment option for kids and only seems to be growing. With that in mind, what should we know about YouTube? And what kind of impact can it have on us and our children?

The Website of Everything

First, let's talk about how YouTube's large selection of videos has propelled it to prominence. As of August 2022, YouTube boasted the second-most traffic of any site on the internet (second only to Google Search, which, as a browser, gains a portion of its traffic from people using it to access YouTube). To give you a reference point for that statistic, the most visited streaming service, Netflix, came in seventeenth. Furthermore, as of 2019, YouTube's most popular channels (nearly forty-four thousand of them with at least two hundred fifty thousand subscribers) account for at least fourteen billion views each week alone.[21]

When we see numbers like these, it's not hard to understand how YouTube's appeal comes from its vast assortment of content. Think of it this way: If Hulu had every show you've ever loved on every topic you've ever cared to watch, it would be hard to justify spending time on any other streaming service. When it comes to YouTube's charms, the choice for many is simple: either spend an hour searching for something on a streaming service that might not be that good and requires a dedicated time commitment *or* view the newest weekly ten-minute upload from your favorite YouTuber on a topic you almost always enjoy.

Still don't believe that YouTube has a channel out there that appeals to your interests? Consider these statistics: According to Statista, as of 2022, YouTube reported that more than five hundred hours' worth of video content was uploaded to the site every *minute*.[22] These videos spanned hundreds of genres and topics—beauty tips, cooking, gaming, history, how-tos, music, news, pranks, product reviews, politics, religion, science, sports, technology, vehicles, and much, *much* more (video games, vehicles, and food-centric videos were the most viewed videos of all subjects).[23] There's even an entire YouTube community based on building aquariums. If you can think of a subject, there's more than likely at least one video on the topic.

While this can mean that your boring day can be filled with

a few interesting videos to help pass the time, it also means that your family could stumble upon myriad videos that are inappropriate for them. Though YouTube age-restricts videos containing adult themes such as violence, sensual images, and heavy swearing (which means that users under eighteen or those without an official account cannot view them), it's still quite easy to bypass this restriction. Users can simply create a new YouTube account and lie about their age, for instance.

Inappropriate content can still land right in your child's lap. With so much new content uploading to the site every second, how could it not? And no filter will screen for issues that might be big problems for *your* family.

Videos may discuss topics inappropriate for your kids or contain ideas that are antithetical to your family's beliefs. They can be full of foul language. Though nudity *technically* isn't allowed on YouTube, some videos include it anyway, and clothing that leaves nothing to the imagination is pretty common. Other videos may contain gore or frightening imagery, such as uploaded clips of horror movies.

YouTube's mission is to "give everyone a voice and show them the world."[24] The website has certainly been able to accomplish that. In fact, it's so chock-full of videos that if you were to begin watching from birth and not stop until death, you'd barely make a dent. This also means that problematic videos and channels might slip past your radar undetected for your kids to discover. We'll talk about how to protect your children from inappropriate content on YouTube in a moment, but first let's investigate another factor that has contributed to YouTube's enormous success.

YouTubers and Identity

The second (and arguably more influential) factor that has boosted YouTube's popularity over the years is the thousands upon thousands of people who create YouTube content.

But before we dive into that topic, let's first set the scene. Do you wonder whether *Plugged In* is just wasting time writing reviews for YouTube channels? How many kids actually use YouTube? Well, according to many reports, the answer is a resounding *lots*—more than any other social media site by far.

For instance, in a 2022 survey, the Pew Research Center found that 95 percent of US teens had used the site.[25] The next highest-ranking social media outlets—TikTok, Instagram, and Snapchat—saw significantly less usage among teens: 67 percent, 62 percent, and 59 percent, respectively. And of the teens who used YouTube, a respectable-yet-concerning one in five of them reported that they visited the site or its app "almost constantly." Seventy-seven percent said they used the website daily.

Common Sense Media found similar results in 2021, reporting that 64 percent of tweens and 77 percent of teens reported daily online video consumption. With 95 percent of teens choosing YouTube as their preferred video platform, it's easy to see which website these kids are flocking to each day. The Common Sense Media survey also found that nearly one in three wouldn't want to live without YouTube.[26]

When children hop onto YouTube, they're not just doing it to find videos on their favorite topics or personal hobbies. They're also using it to connect with the content creators.

A Think with Google analysis reported that 70 percent of teenage YouTube subscribers "relate to YouTube creators more than traditional celebrities."[27] Additionally, the United Kingdom's communications regulator Ofcom found that 46 percent of thirteen-to-seventeen-year-olds used "influencers" to help them feel happy, and 41 percent used them to relax.[28]

So what's the concern about charismatic YouTubers? Well, it's that children are building bonds with online personalities they don't really know who may not be good influences on them. These connections often go beyond casual online relationships. As one research article noted, "Not only did tweens want to be like their favorite YouTuber, they also reported experiencing feelings of friendship." In fact, they even followed their favorite YouTubers "across social media platforms other than YouTube."[29] That might not seem like a concern, especially if the YouTuber is someone you approve of. But it certainly would be a concern if your children begin acting like YouTubers you wouldn't want them emulating.

What Can We Do?

Don't get me wrong. YouTube can be fun, and it can even be—dare I say—a nice way to unwind at the end of the day. I have to confess that I've got my own favorite YouTubers, and I'd be lying if I said I didn't get a little excited each time my phone tells me they've uploaded a new video.

But it's important to teach our children to approach

YouTube the way we approach the internet and entertainment as a whole. There's a plethora of things online that are immensely helpful and good to enjoy, but there are also things online that we shouldn't be messing with. Teaching our children to choose the good while steering clear of the bad will keep them safer as they navigate YouTube and other sites.

Sometimes, though, we know our kids simply need some boundaries to help them stay on the good path. YouTube allows users to make a YouTube Kids or supervised account, both of which automatically filter out many inappropriate videos, allow for screen-time limits, and even grant parents the option to block the ability to search for new videos. However, parents should know this option doesn't block all concerning content, such as videos regarding LGBT topics.

You might also consider purchasing monitoring software. Plenty of services would love to help you monitor your children's internet usage, including their use of YouTube. Focus on the Family—*Plugged In*'s parent ministry—even partners with one. But keep in mind that no monitoring software is perfect.

Most importantly, as parents we should not just monitor our children's YouTube consumption. We also need to foster relationships with our kids so that we can talk about the things they see on the site. That might mean allowing your children to use YouTube only when you can watch videos with them, or perhaps letting them access the site only on a family computer in plain sight.

Asking these questions will help you guide your children in their YouTube viewing:

- What is the point of this video? ("Just for fun" is an okay response too!)
- What messages are being conveyed in this YouTuber's videos?
- Why do you like this YouTuber? Do they act in a way you should emulate? Why or why not?

YouTube is a big space. It can be daunting to dive into, and we can feel overwhelmed as we try to figure out how to navigate it safely. But as the parent, you don't need to analyze every channel; instead, focus on the ones your children gravitate toward, and build communication with them around those channels.

WRAPPING UP (PAUL ASAY)

So which of these forms of entertainment is the most important and influential, you ask? *All of them.* It depends on who you are. We're all so different. God made us that way. As such, we're wired to absorb information, entertainment, and the stories around us in sometimes radically different ways.

That brings up a really important point: Your kids are wired just as differently. So it's absolutely critical that you learn how each one is built. Understanding that deceptively simple element can help you lead and teach your children how to swim in this sometimes bewildering entertainment environment of ours.

And heads up: It's only going to get more bewildering. One of the frustrating things about the world in which *Plugged In* swims is how quickly it can change. When I started working here in 2007—which, honestly, doesn't feel that long ago—MySpace was the big name in social media. (Facebook was the cool new kid, but with less than half of MySpace's traffic.) Netflix was still primarily mailing out DVDs. And, for the most part, screens weren't in our pockets; they were in our living rooms.

That world feels about as archaic to your kids as the horse-and-buggy days feel to us. And the pace of change is only speeding up. We can't anticipate what new advances might be on the horizon in the world of entertainment in ten years, or five, or even by the time you pick up this book. With each new technological leap forward, with each new way to absorb the latest show or video or game, or whatever might be on its way, parents have new challenges to face and new problems to face down.

But the good news is this: You're not alone. Whatever the worlds of entertainment and technology throw at us, *Plugged In* will be with you in some form, whether it be this book, the website, or some other manifestation. And we'll do whatever we can to help, every step of the way.

The Technology Curve

Emily Tsiao

*Technological society has succeeded
in multiplying the opportunities for pleasure,
but it has great difficulty in generating joy.*

POPE PAUL VI

IT'S 1997. I'm five years old. I live in a world without streaming platforms, in a home without a DVR, so if I want to watch my favorite TV show (*Arthur*), I have to wake up before my sisters and beat them to the TV remote. I own a Tamagotchi. My older sister's new Game Boy Pocket is two-dimensional, pixelated, and black-and-white. My parents' Macintosh computer is beige. The World Wide Web has been around for only four years. Connecting to the internet means listening to the dial-up tone for five minutes or more. And mobile phones are still clunky and rare.

It's 2002, and I'm living on a military base in Germany. My school has a computer lab with a teacher dedicated to teaching us how to type, create PowerPoint presentations, and build websites. My favorite thing to do is log on and play Neopets, the internet's version of the Tamagotchi.

It's 2007, and I'm back in the United States attending high school. I'm introduced to Facebook, which has just been launched.

It's 2012. I'm about halfway through college working part-time at one of my school's many computer labs. At this point, professors don't even teach students how to use different computer programs anymore. They just tell them to watch YouTube tutorials online or ask each other.

One of my professors doesn't even do that. I took his class previously, and he knows that I know how the programs work. So rather than try to show his students how to use a program he barely understands, he asks me to demonstrate. And it's not because I'm some sort of computer whiz—*I'm not*—it's because I was born in an age of technology more advanced than his.

It's . . . today. And a lot of people feel like my college professor: behind the technology curve and trying to catch up. And if you're a mom or dad trying to care for a tech-savvy kid, the challenge can be daunting.

The vast majority of parents say that "parenting is harder today than it was 20 years ago" because of technology.[1] And while I personally haven't done any professional studies on the matter, I can say the number one complaint I hear from adults about technology is that it's moving along too quickly to keep up. But rather than roll my eyes and show them how "easy" it is, like I used to, I find myself joining the throng—perhaps for the first time.

It seems the older I get, the faster technology changes. Smartphones and apps update on a near-daily basis. It feels like I don't know half the things my phone is capable of. And I can't help but ask myself, *What's the point of learning about all the cool things my particular smartphone can do if Silicon Valley is going to release a new version with new features in just a few months?*

It's a valid question. And there may not be one right answer. But it's a topic I hope to offer insight on in this chapter.

Seriously, what's the point?

My husband's grandmother is ninety years old. English is her third language. But every piece of technology she owns operates in English. If you want to talk about how annoying it is to adjust to new phone updates, think about how she must feel.

My brother-in-law visits her house at least once a month to provide tech support. He dumbs down the features on her devices so that all she has are the basics. She can call her sons and grandchildren, send emails, and browse the internet. But if one of those three things doesn't work the way she expects it to, she *hates* it.

Why did it change? There was nothing wrong with how it worked before, she argues.

She's not wrong. But technology is changing all the time, and there's nothing she (or we) can do to stop it. She suffers through it for one reason: *us*.

She wants to be able to communicate with her grandkids. She loves getting photo updates of her great-grandbaby. And if that means making a modicum of effort to learn a technology that is foreign to her generation—even more so to her, considering the language barrier—she'll do it.

And that's what the point is.

Yes, it's really annoying when big tech companies release a new smartphone or tablet so soon after introducing the previous one. And yeah, dealing with software updates often makes us scratch our heads (and that's probably putting it nicely for some of us). But we keep up with it because, while we might not see a need for change, the kids in our lives are keeping up with it. And we need to protect them.

Maybe the constantly changing world of technology wouldn't be so bad if the threats of technology weren't so overt. After all, there would be no need for parents to keep up with tech if it were *completely* safe.

Now, I'm not saying that technology is inherently bad. I don't think anybody would argue that *all* tech is *all* bad. We use it for everything from basic communication and research to performing complex, life-saving medical procedures and traveling to the moon and back.

It keeps us safe, and it keeps us connected. But it also has some serious pitfalls.

"Technology can be our best friend, and technology can also be the biggest party pooper of our lives," says director Steven Spielberg. "It interrupts our own story, interrupts our ability to have a thought or a daydream, to imagine something wonderful, because we're too busy bridging the walk from the cafeteria back to the office on the cell phone."[2]

The Pew Research Center has found that most teens use

their cell phones simply to pass the time or connect with others.[3] But several studies have linked frequent screen time to a substantial increase in depression and suicidal thoughts in teens.[4] And while many of these same studies cite social media as the primary offender,[5] evidence shows that sexting and all-too-easily-accessible pornography are factors as well.[6]

When you consider that a staggering 95 percent of all teens living in the US have access to a smartphone, it's not surprising that 46 percent say they use the internet "almost constantly" and that most of them have viewed porn online by the age of seventeen.[7] These statistics really put into perspective how many kids are suffering from their tech use. It also makes the dilemma of whether we should bother trying to keep up with technology even more frustrating. *After all, what sane reason is there to continue using products we know are bad for our health?*

One reason is all the positives I've already mentioned: Tech is cool. It's useful. It's educational. It's entertaining. But perhaps there's a more compelling reason to continue using tech: for the sake of our kids. Tech is incredibly addictive, and as parents, we need to equip our teens to avoid this pitfall.

Social media algorithms are literally designed to keep users scrolling indefinitely.[8] (No wonder so many teens say it would be hard to give it up.) Shopping websites, such as Amazon and Instacart, advertise products related to the ones you've already added to your cart. Streaming platforms like YouTube and Netflix keep people watching by automatically queuing up the next video.

And while most studies have focused on kids, we here at *Plugged In* know that adults are just as vulnerable to the negative effects of technology.[9] Which means we need to understand how it works and how it's designed to keep us hooked if we're going to have any chance of helping our kids navigate these dangers.

So *how* do we protect our kids?

Surprisingly, keeping up with technology—and setting up boundaries to protect our kids from its negative effects—isn't all that complicated. You don't need to be an IT expert to implement some safe technology habits. (Though it can certainly *feel* that way given the vast amount of knowledge on the topic that's available online.)

But after doing a fair bit of research into the matter myself, I've found that it boils down to a few simple practices.

Delay Your Kids' Engagement with Technology

Keeping our kids away from technology is a bit paradoxical in nature. On the one hand, the longer we wait to expose them to screens, the less likely they'll be to develop mental-health issues.[10] On the other, the closer kids get to the tween and teenage years, the more likely they are to be mocked for *not* having the latest gadgets and gizmos—and being constantly left out comes with its own share of issues.

When it comes to delaying your child's entry into the tech world, you might have some surprising company: tech experts. Many tech-company executives have raised their own children in a completely tech-free (or seriously tech-limited) environment to shield them from the psychological dangers of technology.[11]

So how young is too young for tech use?

Well, pediatric research tells us that using a screen as a digital pacifier for babies can actually stunt their social development—but only if used too frequently.[12] So if you use your phone to calm your screaming child in the grocery store on occasion, you're probably not harming them. But if you set them in front of a television for multiple hours a day, they'll learn to seek out the immediate gratification of screens over the slower (but more meaningful) interactions in the real world.[13]

Health experts recommend that children under the age of five should have no more than one hour of screen time each day—and "less is even better."[14] So buying young children a device seems impractical and unnecessary. Jonathan McKee, a tech and family expert who shares his knowledge on our own *Plugged In Show*, notes that most experts say that parents should hold off on letting their kids have a phone until at least age thirteen.[15]

Studies show that as kids get older, digital devices can actually help them develop friendships. According to a Pew survey, more than half of all teens use digital devices to communicate with their friends on a daily basis.[16] Most teens feel that social media (and, for boys, video games) helps them stay more connected to friends and peers.

So delaying the use of technology indefinitely, while admirable, may not be as beneficial for our kids as we might hope. But the longer you can wait, the better.

Limit the Time Spent on Screens

Once you've made the decision to allow your children to use technology, the next best thing you can do is limit *when*, *where*, and *how much*.

Excessive screen time and "regular exposure to poor-quality programming" have been linked to obesity, insufficient sleep, behavioral problems, developmental delays in language and social skills, attention problems, and even violence, says the Mayo Clinic.[17] But if you implement screen-time restrictions for your family, including where your kids can use their devices and for how long, you greatly reduce these risks.

Consider creating tech-free times, such as during family dinners. Research has shown that eating meals together sans screens can actually help reduce stress, depression, and anxiety.[18] You could even institute tech-free zones in your house too. For instance, people often gather in the kitchen after school or work to have a snack or make dinner or just decompress after an active day. Lots of organic conversations can start in the kitchen, so making yours a phone-free zone might just inspire those conversations to bloom.

When your kids are studying or doing homework, turn off the TV in the background and turn on some classical music. Reports have indicated for a while now that playing classical music in the background while studying can aid retention. It can also reduce stress levels and promote healthier sleep patterns.[19]

Think about taking technology out of your family's bedrooms, too. A *Forbes* article observed that screen brightness can cause us to feel more alert, which makes it harder to fall asleep at night.[20] So remove the TVs from everyone's bedrooms and swap the smartphones for alarm clocks.

Furthermore, common sense tells us that allowing our teens to take their laptops or cell phones into their rooms impedes our ability to monitor their screen usage. By eliminating the option, we naturally gain a level of control that allows us to observe how our children use their devices and whether that behavior is acceptable.

Finally, create a screen-time limit. One study found that intentionally reducing phone usage by just one hour each day resulted in healthier phone habits after the study was completed. That same research also saw reductions in anxiety, depression, and nicotine use for those who limited their screen time.[21]

If screen-time limits are difficult to enforce in your home, use parental control features to set the limit for you. (More on that later.)

Research before You Buy a Device or Download an App

Just as you wouldn't buy a car without checking the cost, brand reliability, features, and customer reviews, you shouldn't buy a device without doing the same.

Does the device you're considering have parental controls? What are the limitations of those? Can you download a specific third-party app or software program to help monitor activity? Do users frequently run into problems while setting up parental controls? How easy is it for kids to disable the controls? And will the installation and implementation of these features affect the device's overall performance?

Not all devices are created the same. Some companies are more dedicated than others in their efforts to ensure safe user experiences. They provide parental controls that block websites, filter content, set time limits, and track location. Other companies, fearful of diminishing the user's experience (and perhaps prioritizing profits over consumer safety), limit how much control parents have or disregard the concept altogether.

But a device's exclusion of parental controls doesn't necessarily mean you shouldn't purchase it. Many third-party apps allow parents to do all the things I just mentioned and more. You can see the websites your kids are visiting and the apps they're using. You can monitor their text messages and social media profiles. You'll also be alerted if your kids use certain words.

And if you're worried that your teen will think you're being crazy, rest assured that you aren't the only concerned parent. A Pew Research Center survey found that nearly three in four parents use parental controls to check younger kids' online activity and restrict how much they use screens.[22]

Speaking of which . . .

Utilize Those Parental Controls and Know Your Kids' Passwords

Once you've found a device (and perhaps some additional software or apps) that meets your standards for parental controls, *don't forget to enable them.*

Not to throw my parents under the bus, but they *never* utilized technical parental controls (although they did take away my Nintendo DS a few times when I failed to do my chores). In fairness to them, I don't think many parents did back then. If I got a new gaming console or phone, I was allowed to pull it out of the box, take it to a private area, and start it up for the first time on my own.

Nobody knew my usernames and passwords but me. My parents had no idea what I did on my computer or what I watched on TV. And since they never bothered to check my browsing history, I was perfectly positioned to get away with whatever I wanted.

Granted, I was kind of a Goody-Two-Shoes, and the most questionable things I ever did were watch *Whose Line Is It Anyway?* late on school nights and spend too much time building houses on *The Sims*.

Even if your children aren't using their devices for nefarious deeds, you should still know some basic things about their screen usage, since they're vulnerable to the negative effects of overuse, oversharing, and cyberbullying. A majority of parents share these concerns.[23]

Experts recommend using device-monitoring software if you suspect that your child is bullying or being bullied online. Additionally, by knowing your children's usernames and passwords, you can personally check for red flags in their posts or messages.[24]

If you're worried that your children are simply spending too much time online, that's one of the easier fixes. Many devices have built-in features that allow you to track how much time is spent across different apps and put specific limits on the ones you choose. Some devices can also be set to stop working altogether if the user goes over the screen limit.

So set some boundaries. Make sure your kids know what the expectation is. And don't be afraid to take away their devices if they abuse their privileges. (You won't be alone. According to a Pew survey, 80 percent of parents say they've taken away their child's cell phone or internet privileges as a punishment.[25])

If you need help getting started with parental controls, there are many tutorials available online (including some published by *Plugged In*) that can teach you step by step how to use them.

Stay Digitally Aware

I've already mentioned how important it is for us to be aware of how technology works and how it's designed to keep its users hooked. So what better way to figure that out than to test it yourself?

Set up the parental controls on a device you're considering for your children and then see how they work. Max out the time limit. Try to access a blocked website. Check to see if the filter is working.

Then take it a step further.

Look up the loopholes for parental controls. If you know the different ways your kids might try to get around or even disable the controls you've set up, you'll be more likely to notice it if they do.

There are apps and computer programs designed to help people hide content they don't want others to see. Some even automatically delete evidence of online activity. Others can scramble GPS signals to make tracking ineffective.

I knew a guy who learned how to hide the shortcut for a computer game he wasn't allowed to play, and he did it in plain sight on his parents' desktop computer. Essentially, he made the icon invisible. And the only way it could be accessed was if the user knew *exactly* where it was located on the screen.

Other people I know have gotten around phone-monitoring software by using browsers hidden within social media apps or by purchasing a "burner" phone.

A simple web search can alert you to these methods. It can also tell you which apps are used for bypassing parental controls and what they look like. While you're browsing, take a minute to look up the most recent digital trends for adolescents (or subscribe to some tech bloggers and vloggers who can tell you all about it).

These trends can change on a weekly or even a *daily* basis, so you probably won't catch them all. But it can help you to be mindful of the types of activities and worldviews that are being promoted to teens through the technology they use.

Model Good Behavior for Digital Use

Plugged In's Adam Holz once wrote, "As parents, it's tempting to say, 'Do as I say, not as I do.' But if our kids see us using social media compulsively or addictively, they're more likely to pay attention to what we actually *do* than what we *say*."[26]

Honestly, I could end this section right there. But I'll back it up with some stats from the Pew Research Center:

- Nearly six in ten US parents report feeling obligated to respond *immediately* to messages on their cell phones.
- Thirty-nine percent of parents say they "regularly lose focus at work because they're checking their mobile device."
- Thirty-six percent of parents admit to spending too much time on their screens.[27]

Just because we're adults doesn't mean we're immune to the dangers of technology. I've personally had to delete certain gaming apps on my smartphone because of how distracting they were. I've also deleted certain social media accounts after I realized how negatively they were affecting my mental health. And even within the past month, I had to implement the screen-time controls on my smartphone because I would get on to read a news article or look something up and wind up spending *hours* browsing through clickbaity articles.

It's important to remember that *we* control the technology, not the other way around. And if we, as the *adults*, need to monitor our digital behavior, then it's all the more important to set a good example for younger generations.

Any other pieces of advice?

Just one: *Talk to your kids about all this.*

Steve Jobs, the cofounder of Apple, once said that "technology is nothing. What's important is that you have a faith in people, that they're basically good and smart, and if you give them tools, they'll do wonderful things with them."[28]

I don't agree.

As Christians, we know that we are all sinners in need of a Savior. And while people certainly *can* do wonderful things with technology, the only reason this chapter exists is because many people—even those who have accepted the redemption of Jesus Christ—*haven't*.

Between cyberbullying, sexting, online pornography, burner phones, hacking, identity theft, digital conglomerate whistleblowers, and a branch of the internet so awful that we've collectively come to know it as the "dark web," I don't have a lot of faith that people will use technology for good.

However, I *do* have faith that we as Christian parents can learn how to navigate the nastier side effects of technology and teach our kids to do the same. By keeping the lines of communication open, we can better understand how our kids use technology. We can also have discussions with them about healthy digital behaviors and figure out what methods of parental controls (whether technical or practical) are most effective.

Most importantly, we can develop and foster a *relationship* with our kids that will allow us to mentor them through this digital age even as they continue to teach us about all the new technological advances we've failed to keep up with.

PART 4

It's Not All Bad

10

The Reset

Adam R. Holz

I'M NOT A SCIENTIST. (I don't even play one on TV.) But sometimes you remember things you learned in a science class because they make so much sense.

Take, for example, the second law of thermodynamics. Essentially, this rule recognizes that things tend toward chaos, decay, and disorder unless outside energy is invested to restore order. Without that energy being injected into the system from the outside, *entropy*—total chaos in which all the existing energy within a system has been expended—will rule.

I often ponder the second law of thermodynamics—at least, the way I remember it from eighth-grade physics. Because, let's face it, *order never happens accidentally*. Order is the by-product of intentionality and energy being expended to take something that's out of whack and set it right again. It implies, by its very definition, *work*.

We see this dynamic in virtually every area of our lives. Leave dirty dishes on the counter before work, and they're still going to be there when you get home if no one has invested outside energy in restoring order. Dishes don't magically clean themselves. (What a miracle that would be, right?) Leave them a couple of days, and bugs start showing up. (Ask me how I know—I was single until I was thirty-four.) More chaos. I suspect you could leave your dishes for a thousand years, and they'd still be dirty (though probably worth more at that point, now that they're archaeological relics).

I think something like the second law of thermodynamics is at play in our character and moral core too. We move naturally from order toward disorder, a consequence of the Fall. Left to our own devices, without God's redemptive input in our lives, we drift toward self-gratification pretty naturally. That's true of our interaction with screens and technology too.

Even if we've set good boundaries (as we talked about earlier) and worked hard to protect them, our screen-based interactions can easily follow the same pattern: from discipline to undiscipline, order to chaos. Like the movie *Groundhog Day*, in which Bill Murray relives the same day over and over, it's easy to end up in a spot where we realize, *I've been here before*.

In my family, we do try to keep some semblance of entertainment and tech order. One of our rules is not to engage with two screens at once. If you're focusing on multiple screens, after all, you're probably not focusing on any of them. And you might be missing something important. That's especially true if you're engaging with a screen with other people—during a family movie night, for instance.

Recently we were having a family movie night. I honestly don't remember what we were watching, but I do remember that my middle daughter soon busted me. Without my even being aware, my hand had drifted to my phone, and I was somewhat mindlessly scrolling when she yelled at me, "Dad! No dual-screening! Put your phone down!"

Point taken. She was reminding me of one of our family screen guidelines that I was, in fact, breaking. I had drifted outside the boundaries we've tried to establish as a family.

Now, that was just one choice. One moment. But it was a telling one, a sign that my own relationship with technology had drifted noticeably. And I realized it was probably time for a family screen reset—even if I was the one who needed it most right at that moment.

HOUSTON, WE HAVE A PROBLEM

We all know that setting boundaries on screen-time use is hugely important for the sake of our kids' mental, emotional, and spiritual health. (And ours, too!)

But if we're being honest as parents, sometimes our grip slips. We implement new habits, we make changes, we see progress with regard to how we're spending time—or not spending time—with screens. And then—*bam!*—Christmas break happens. Someone gets sick. Or something else disrupts our schedule, and our kids begin to stumble back into old habits. It could be something as maddeningly mundane as a really stressful week or two. And suddenly, our family's screen-time usage is out of control again.

In those moments, it can be tempting to throw in the towel, to feel like the hard work of setting limits and making healthy changes is just unrealistic. Or, worse, impossible. *What's the point?* we might wonder dejectedly. *We're just going to end up in the same place again. Why fight it?* Indeed, the impulse to throw in the towel here can be disturbingly strong. If you can't beat 'em, join 'em, right? The pull of passivity—a pull that almost always leads to disorder—is like that.

But the fact is, setting limits is hard in any area of our lives. Anyone who's ever tried to redirect old habits and establish healthy, new ones knows it's anything but easy. And I'd suggest that the same is true when it comes to making changes to our family's screen-time usage.

When things slip out of control, it's time for a screen-time reset. So how do we do that? And how do we move toward making changes stick?

Mission Drift

Even though we know better, it's easy to drift off course. (Remember: entropy!) For many of us, our smartphones are also our alarm clocks—the first thing we reach for in the morning and the last thing we interact with before we go to sleep. It's no wonder we can find ourselves using them perhaps more than we intend.

Toss in the fact that social media developers spend a lot of time making sure we're never out of the loop, and we have a situation in which this truly spectacular technology threatens at times to take over every waking minute of our—and our children's—lives, if we let it.

In the 2020 documentary *The Social Dilemma*, former Google designer Tristan Harris, who now sounds the alarm about the product he used to create, said, "Every time you see [your phone] there on the counter and just look at it. And you know if you reach over, it just might have something for you. So you play that slot machine to see what you got. That's not by accident. That's a design technique."

Former Pinterest president Tim Kendall added, "[The business model of] companies like [Facebook, Twitter, YouTube, and Instagram] is to keep people engaged on the screen. Let's figure out how to get as much of this person's attention as we possibly can. How much time can we get you to spend? How much of your life can we get you to give to us?"[1]

Wow. It's a lot to consider. As if steering clear of bad tech habits wasn't hard enough. We're not just talking about resisting and saying no to something that's benign and neutral here. Instead, we're talking about setting limits on a system that's actively trying to get us—and our children—to cede as much of our waking attention as they can get. It's a sobering thought, and it helps explain why trying to break these habits when they *do* cycle out of control can seem so difficult.

Difficult, but not impossible. So what do we do in those moments where there's more chaos than order, more caving in than carving out space without our beloved screens.

In those moments, it's time for a reset. Let's talk about what that is and what it might entail for your family.

Reset Reloaded

A reset is a renewed commitment to look at our technology boundaries and adjust them to bring more order and health into our relationships with screens. There's no "right" way to do it (though I'll offer a bunch of concrete suggestions later in this chapter). But it does involve acknowledging that your family's habits are out of whack in this area and working together to reset what your relationships with screens, technology, and entertainment should look like.

However, before we even begin to implement some of those changes, we've got to be honest and realistic about what we're dealing with.

As we discovered earlier in this book, changing habits in entertainment isn't an overnight process. Making healthy changes stick involves more than just ramping up our willpower, as important as that is. We've got to realize that our screen habits condition our brains in a very real way to want the stimulation that all those flickering pixels promise. We need to understand that our brains crave the dopamine hit looking at our screens gives us: It's an appetite and an addiction.

That's why making changes can feel painful at first. In fact, I'd suggest that resetting our screen habits is akin to two other practices most of us have done at some point: dieting and budgeting. Neither is particularly easy or pleasant. But the outcomes—better health and more financial security— are worth the effort.

There's an inescapable element of discipline here, but the outcome is a fruitful one, as the author of Hebrews reminds us: "For the moment all discipline seems painful rather than pleasant, but later it yields the peaceful fruit of righteousness to those who have been trained by it" (Hebrews 12:11, ESV). Discipline is rarely easy or natural. Saying no to ourselves costs us something in the moment—namely, that brief, immediate gratification. But in the end, consistently applying it helps us move in the direction we ultimately want to go.

Parents, You Go First

If you've ever flown on a commercial flight, you've heard safety procedures that might at first blush seem counterintuitive: Parents are supposed to put their oxygen masks on first in the event of an emergency and then help their children do the same.

There's a parallel principle in play when it comes to dealing with screen time in the family. Parents, we need to get our proverbial houses in order first. It's easy and perhaps natural to make our kids' screen usage our top priority. But the reality is this: Our kids are likely just doing what we're doing as parents. They don't have to try to emulate us; they just do it.

So first, Mom and Dad, we need to take a look in the mirror. How much are you on your phone? What changes do *you* need to begin making before you ask your kids to change their own habits? It may seem like their issues are more pressing, but I guarantee you that they'll be watching you. And "Do as I say, not as I do" will not work here.

One change I've been *trying* to make (see how I hedged there? This isn't easy!) is to turn off my phone for two hours every evening. That enables me to come home from work and be fully present with my kids and wife instead of being sucked into the ever-present vortex of "content" via my smartphone.

That's been a good starting place for me when it comes to leading a successful reset. And that brings me to my next point.

Rejecting All-or-Nothing Thinking and Perfectionism

How do you tend to go about making changes in your life? Do you typically make one small adjustment and then another until the desired course correction has been achieved? Or do you go at it full force, determined to make massive changes in one fell swoop?

I confess, I tend to be in the latter category. Like some gigantic Paul Bunyan swinging an ax the size of a pickup truck, I take aim with all my might at a given problem, hoping to fell it with one decisive blow.

If you're wondering how that works—well, generally speaking, it doesn't. Oh, there can be a lot of noise and pyrotechnics, figuratively speaking. But we don't make lasting changes or solve complex problems with a single grand gesture. Instead, change is built on small adjustments that we integrate over time. In military terms, we might think of it as reclaiming lost territory, one battle at a time. The war isn't won overnight. But if we persist, we'll look back and realize we've retaken a lot of lost ground.

A recent study by researchers at Ruhr-Universität Bochum in Germany backs up this approach to making changes stick when it comes to tech's place in our lives. Scientists divided 619 study participants into three groups. The first group was asked to abstain completely from their phones for a full week—the cold-turkey approach. The other group was tasked with reducing their phone usage by one hour a day but otherwise interacting with their devices the way they normally would. The third group made no adjustments at all in limiting their smartphone use. Researchers then checked in with participants a month into the study, and then four months later.

Who do you think used their phones less after this study? Obviously, I've telegraphed the findings already: The group that cut usage by an hour a day over a week were still using their phones, on average, thirty-eight fewer minutes per day four months later. In contrast, those who went cold turkey drifted back into more usage more quickly.[2]

Lead researcher Dr. Julia Brailovskaia summarized the study's findings: "We found that both completely giving up the smartphone and reducing its daily use by one hour had positive effects on the lifestyle and well-being of the participants. . . . In the group who reduced use, these effects even lasted longer and were thus more stable than in the abstinence group."[3]

I love that study. Instead of all-or-nothing perfectionism, I think it shows us that the opposite is the best strategy for the long haul. The goal isn't absolute perfection or instantaneous change. The goal is movement toward what is healthy and good for us. Sometimes we blow it—just like with a diet, or a budget. But we don't quit. Instead, we reset, regroup, and try again.

Replacement Theory

Now, we need to talk about another important consideration: what we're filling that vacated digital space with. Here's what I mean.

When I'm trying to make changes, I often get very intense about what I intend to *give up*, to cut out. But my wise wife always asks the corollary question: *What are you going to fill that empty space with?* That's a great question. Because the truth is, it's hard to eliminate anything we like without a concrete plan for replacing it with something that offers a different kind of satisfaction.

For us as parents, resetting our kids' screen-time limits demands something more than just a parental edict that we're not going to do *X* anymore. When we remove something from our children's lives that they enjoy and are used to doing, it's going to create a vacuum we have a responsibility to help them fill. That requires planning and intentionality. (There's the word *intentionality* again!)

For our family, we've tried to find things we like to do together. There are several games all of us enjoy (or, well, most of us, most of the time), as well as certain shared activities. So if I say, "It's time to get off your phone," that instruction is much easier for my kids to take if I have a replacement activity in mind. With my son, for instance, I might suggest "So let's go play guitar together" or "Show me a guitar lick you've learned this week." He and I enjoy making music together, whereas my wife and daughters are more likely to enjoy doing puzzles and various craftsy things together. Or, during volleyball season, heading out to the backyard to practice their bumps, sets, and spikes.

We also sometimes have fun contests, especially on breaks. *Who can read the most pages (and/or books) over a break?* Or we have a drawing contest where each family member comes up with a category of objects to sketch out: The best tree, for instance, or the best animal, or the best Millennium Falcon (I wish).

Your family's replacement strategies may look very different from mine. In fact, they probably will, because they should be built on whatever you and your kids enjoy doing or have an aptitude for. But the point is this: We're not just dropping screen-time regulations on our kids from on high and expecting them to naturally know what to do with the empty space we've just created. Instead, we're actively and intentionally engaged as parents in brainstorming and modeling non–screen-related activities. And the more we help our children choose those activities, the more likely they are to make those wise choices without our close guidance and encouragement to do so.

PUSHING THE RESET BUTTON: LOOK FOR A NATURAL RESET POINT

So how do we get started when it comes to actually initiating the kind of reset I've been talking about?

It's not impossible to make changes right in the middle of your normal schedule. Like, say, starting on a random Wednesday morning. But in my family's experience, it's a bit easier to do that when there's a natural reset point.

It can be as simple as the next weekend or the next break from school (fall break, Christmas break, spring break, or the beginning of summer). These sorts of breaks offer natural transition points where reintegrating renewed boundaries feels less jarring.

So if things are starting to feel a bit frazzled, you can get out your calendar right now and ask, "What's the next best spot for our family to reset our media habits?"

Baby Steps: Small, Measurable, Achievable Changes

At the risk of sounding like I'm a Bill Murray fanboy (which I'm really not), I want to mention another famous role of his. In the 1991 movie *What about Bob?*,[4] Murray plays a man named Bob Wiley who struggles with crippling phobias that can make even basic, everyday-life stuff difficult for him. His therapist, Dr. Leo Marvin (played by Richard Dreyfuss), suggests that meaningful change begins with "baby steps."

"Baby steps?" Bob asks.

"It means setting small, reasonable goals for yourself one day at a time. One tiny step at a time. Baby steps," Dr. Marvin replies.

For a mainstream comedy, there's a lot of practical wisdom wrapped up in Dr. Marvin's counsel. Taking "baby steps," one after another, can change our family's trajectory, one little step at a time.

So what might that look like? Let me offer a few concrete ideas that echo or build upon others we've seen so far throughout this book. Consider these suggestions:

Buy an alarm clock. Yes, we'll say this again. Just go do it. Now. And while you're at it, get one for each of your kids, too. This means that instead of your phone being the first and last thing you have contact with each day, you can do something truly old-fashioned that only people in the movies do now: turn off your annoying, buzzing alarm clock.

No phone before breakfast. It's so easy to pick up our phones the second we wake up, as I mentioned above. But there's a growing body of research that suggests we should abstain from them for at least the first hour after waking because they instantly kick our brains into a state of alertness (which sounds good) that can create anxiety and stress (there's the rub). So consider embracing a boundary that puts your phone out of reach for that critical first hour of consciousness. Many who've reported doing so say, anecdotally, that they have less stress and are more productive in their lives as a result.

No phones at dinner. We've already mentioned this in chapter 9, but it's worth repeating, in part because it might be the easiest place to start. When your family eats together, put the phones away. Admittedly, many families may not eat together more than once or twice a week. But doing so has enormous benefits, because it's a place where kids usually begin to talk about how their lives are going. So if you're eating, get a phone basket and put 'em away.

The two-hour challenge. Scientists suggest a two-hour screen-time limit for children and adolescents. But we know that most teens (and most adults) are clocking somewhere between six and eight hours of screen time daily. Getting down to two hours is sort of like taking up running and deciding to sign up for marathon a week later. So we've got to reduce our usage in chunks.

May I suggest what I call the two-hour challenge? As I noted earlier, I'm doing my best to turn off my phone for two hours every evening (usually between 6:00 and 8:00 p.m.). It's amazing how just two hours has an impact on my mental clarity. Maybe that's because I'd otherwise be reaching for my phone to check the news, Facebook, my favorite sports teams, and other sites about once every four minutes. That's right: According to a survey of US adults in 2023, most were checking their phones about once every four minutes.[5] Looked at from that perspective, putting your phone away for two hours at a time is no small thing.

The two-hour challenge, part 2. A positive part of putting your phone down for two hours is that, well, you've got two hours back in your life. What might you do with that time? What hobby might you pursue? What relationship might you invest in? What exercise program might you start? The sky's the limit. And if we think about trimming phone use as an opportunity for personal development and growth, this is a great way to start.

Turn off your phone in the car. Should be easy, right? You're *driving*. Still, 27 percent of Americans report looking at their phones while driving.[6] And I suspect a good portion of the other 73 percent aren't telling the truth. If we turn off our phones in the car, we can ask our kids to do the same. Instead of everyone riding to school with AirPods in their ears listening to their own music (ask me how I know), just think: We could have a real conversation with our kids.

Whoever reads the most wins. One summer (and, truth-fully, we only did this once), we had a reading competition in our family (with a generous cash reward for the winner). Now, is offering a monetary prize the best way to encourage your kids to read? I don't know. But I do know we all read a *lot* that summer. So even something as seemingly crass as bribing your kids to put their phones down may be worth considering.

Phones off an hour before bed. Speaking of better sleep, ideally we should all be stowing our little pixelated "preciouses" at least sixty minutes before bed. That's because it takes that long for your brain to unwind to a good rest state. The so-called "blue light" emitted intensely by phones, as well as other screens, essentially awakens the brain to a ready state and makes deep and healthy sleep more difficult.

No phones overnight in bedrooms. What good can come of kids having their phones in their bedrooms overnight? None. There are the obvious issues for parents, such as not knowing how late our kids may be up or what they may be looking at. And then there are the less obvious things, like friends pinging them on social media at 3:34 in the morning and wrecking their sleep. This is another change where the pushback may initially be strong, but ultimately it will help your kids sleep better.

Tech-Free Tuesday. I have to give credit here to my friend Jonathan McKee, author of *Parenting Generation Screen*. He and his family identified one evening a week to turn off the tech devices and do something fun together as a family. Jonathan reports that initially there was big pushback from his kids. But as they got into this tech-free groove, they actually began to look forward to it, even commenting about how much better life was when they put down their phones for an evening.[7] Though the writer in me loves the alliteration in "Tech-Free Tuesday," there's obviously nothing magical about that particular day. Maybe your family can have a "Family-Focused Friday" or even a "Sabbath Saturday" (though you see that I'm still having a hard time letting go of my love affair with alliteration).

Now, remember how I said earlier that the all-or-nothing approach is likely a setup for failure? If you're gung-ho to make changes, you might be tempted to say yes to all these suggestions. But I'd encourage you to pick one change and integrate it into your life for sixty to ninety days; then perhaps choose another one. That kind of slow change will help it stick, as opposed to giving you one really good, amazingly disciplined week before it all falls apart because too much change at once was unsustainable.

WINNING ONE FOR THE HOME TEAM

Change is hard. Making lasting changes to unhealthy or destructive screen habits is no small thing. While one spouse in a marriage may be able to influence the kind of family-culture changes I'm talking about, it's going to be harder if Mom or Dad is going it alone. If possible, getting on the same page with your spouse will vastly increase the likelihood of success in this area. It also creates an opportunity for marital bonding as you both work toward a common goal in this area.

One final word on resets. The world of screens that permeates our lives today isn't going away (well, not short of one of those apocalyptic events we see in dystopian sci-fi movies, that is). It's a reality that anyone raising kids today has to grapple with for the foreseeable future. And that means we're not always going to get it exactly right. Sometimes our habits slip out of control. That's just a part of life.

But our goal doesn't have to be perfection when it comes to media and technology. Rather, our goal is to be engaged and aware of our habits, and to periodically reset them when discipline wanes (because we're tired or sick or had a bad day . . . or week), as it naturally tends to do.

It can feel like a losing battle sometimes—a battle that gets even tougher as kids move into their teen years. That said, I believe that if we stay engaged relationally, continue to set healthy limits, and keep hitting the reset button when we drift outside those boundaries, it will give our kids a model for relating to others and interfacing with technology.

As long as we don't quit trying altogether, I believe our children will reap the benefits of our determination—frayed though it may feel at times—to not give up the media fight but to get back in there again and give it another try.

There's *always* an opportunity for a reset, a chance to start over and keep working on developing healthy boundaries and limits over the long haul.

11

Coming Together

Paul Asay

OVER THE LAST TEN CHAPTERS, we've talked quite a bit about the problems we find in entertainment and technology.

Movies can warp our view of sex.

Scientists have found connections between entertainment violence and real-world violence.

The worldviews we find in entertainment can lead us away from God.

We've also talked about how too much screen time can be unhealthy, how social media can make us depressed, and how the internet itself might be changing our brains.

All that, and much, much more, is true.

And yet, let me let you in on a little secret: I like movies.

I don't like *all* movies. There are a lot of movies I'm paid to see that, well, you'd have to pay me to see. But every year, I review films that make me laugh, make me cry, make me think, and might even help make me a better person.

I could say the same thing for every other entertainment medium we cover at *Plugged In*. Technology, too, can enrich our lives as well as fragment and fracture it. The screens we engage with are—like hammers, cars, and hot stoves—just *tools*. Yes, they can be dangerous, but they can be useful, too. They can enrich our lives. And perhaps most critically, they can strengthen our connections with people. We can use them to bond with our children, with our parents, with people we've never even met. And if we engage with the right stories and think about them as we ought, we might even find ourselves feeling closer to God.

I know, it sounds strange after reading so many pages of how entertainment and technology can separate and isolate us relationally from each other and from God. And yes, we watch TV shows by ourselves on our pocket-sized screens. We shout at each other on social media. In some ways, this tech-driven, entertainment-soaked age of ours has made us feel more alone than ever.

But it doesn't have to be that way. Let me show you a few ways entertainment and technology can bring us closer and help us grow our communities in ways that might surprise you.

ENTERTAINMENT AND TECHNOLOGY
CAN FOSTER COMMUNICATION

Call it the first tweet.

The message was a dainty twenty-two (with spaces) characters. It traveled the distance between Washington, DC, and Baltimore almost instantaneously. And when Samuel Morse sent Alfred Vail the message "What hath God wrought?" over their revolutionary telegraph system in 1844, it upended communication forever.[1]

Messages that had taken weeks to travel could suddenly jump across the country in minutes. And that invention reshaped the world.

We are social creatures. God made us so. We are a people meant for *community*, not isolation. The core of community is, of course, *communication*. And while we've taken huge strides in a lot of scientific fields since Morse sent that first message, I'd argue that no field has pushed into the realm of science fiction as much as how we talk with each other.

Don't believe me? Think about those old episodes of *Star Trek*, produced between 1966 and 1969. Creator Gene Roddenberry was hypothesizing where humankind might be three hundred years into the future back then, and boy, what a world he envisioned. We could cover vast galactic distances at, literally, warp speed. We could move between a starship and a planet by dematerializing in one place and reconstructing all our atoms in another via the ship's transporter. (If only I could transport between Colorado Springs and Denver for movie screenings each week so easily.) Doctors could detect illness just by waving a tiny device over the sick person's body, and food could be conjured practically out of thin air via a replicator (though, admittedly, some thought that replicator dinners were a bit "off" compared to the real thing).

And how did these future people communicate? Through devices that looked an awful lot like old-fashioned flip phones, turning dials sometimes to home in on the signal. No pocket-sized video screens, no internet at their fingertips. While most of *Star Trek*'s technology has yet to come to pass, the way the characters in the show communicated with one another looks positively primitive compared to where we are in the twenty-first century.

And we've still got two hundred years to go.

Roddenberry imagined that we could shrink the galaxy through warp drives. He believed that seeking out new worlds and civilizations would be our primary motivation, that we'd want to go where no one had gone before. And while that might indeed be true, he underestimated how much we wanted—perhaps needed—the worlds we already knew and the people already in them. Galactic exploration is fine and all. But what we really wanted was not a chance to talk to Klingons halfway across the galaxy but a chance to talk to our sisters halfway across the country—and to feel like they're right here with us.

Nothing is more important to us than communication. No wonder we're always coming up with new ways to talk to each other.

The internet itself was created for connection. We now have a dizzying number of social media platforms. YouTube celebrities make their money based on how well they connect with their audience—an audience that can often be made up of millions. And for all the downsides of the communication age, let us not lose sight of its upside.

But, of course, communication is not just about *how* we talk to each other. Let's dig a little deeper and ask *what* we talk *about*. What is one of the first points of connection—even of similarity—that we find in someone we meet?

It's our stories.

SEEING OURSELVES ON-SCREEN

Seen any good movies lately?

It's a question I hear a lot. And while I probably hear it more than most (being a movie reviewer and all), I think perhaps you've heard the question a time or two yourself. Chances are good that the conversations might run deeper than that if they go on for five minutes. Superhero fans might rank the Marvel movies. Teen girls might rank Disney princess movies from their childhoods. Movie wonks like me might argue over the best directors or best actors or, if you're truly wonky, whether Martin Scorsese's best works came before or after *Goodfellas*. We could talk about everything from Alfred Hitchcock's use of color to "Wasn't the last *Top Gun* flick cool?" And, of course, that all filters into the worlds of television and video games and music tracks too. These are often the very first steps in forming a friendship, common ground that paves the way to deeper community.

I'll admit that when I was younger—and more media was displayed on shelves, not hidden in phones—the first thing

I'd do when I went to someone's house was look over their books or CD collections. Did we read the same authors? Did we listen to the same bands? Getting to know someone's entertainment preferences was a shorthand way of getting to know an important part of that person. I'll admit that when I first met my wife-to-be, it felt as if we had nothing in common. And then we started talking about books, and I thought, *She might be okay after all.*

While I think most of us long for real connection—where we can talk about our fears and dreams and meet someone we can call at 4:00 a.m.—most friendships don't begin that way. They begin small, where we talk of things of little consequence but of mutual enjoyment. Sports. Hobbies. Entertainment. Many a fast friendship has begun through a mutual love of Star Wars or *Parks and Recreation* or *Super Smash Bros.*

Entertainment doesn't just allow us to connect with newish friends. It can be used to connect, or reconnect, with family, too. It can mysteriously tie generations together. Consider: A twelve-year-old today has never known a world without the internet. She's always had iPhones, always had YouTube. Now think about that twelve-year-old's grandmother, and her world of corded phones and huge tube TVs. Think about that twelve-year-old's great-grandmother, who might remember a time when most folks didn't have a TV at all and the phone she had was shared with everyone in the vicinity on a "party line." The world has changed a staggering amount in just a few decades—so much so that what was common in the 1960s looks about as archaic now as an ox-drawn plow.

What could a twelve-year-old and an eighty-year-old possibly have in common?

Bambi, that's what.

Entertainment can bridge the staggering gap between generations. And if both parties are willing, it can make that bridge stronger. Those from an older generation can introduce the younger to *Casablanca* and Louis Armstrong. Younger fans just might get their grandparents interested in Taylor Swift or *Mario Kart*. Thus a new experience and shared connection is born, deepening those relational ties further.

And perhaps most important for our purposes, entertainment can help us bond with our own children. It helps us connect with them and even teach them in ways that previous generations never could. Of course, that requires both wisdom and discernment, but the tools are at our fingertips. Let me give you a few examples of how entertainment can be used wisely in our families.

Entertainment Gives Us an Excuse (and Sometimes a Vocabulary) to Talk about Important Things

In 2015, Pixar came out with a movie called *Inside Out*.[2] It focused on a girl named Riley and all the crazy emotions roiling inside her: joy, sadness, anger, fear, disgust. At the beginning of the film, the buoyant emotion Joy wants to run the show. She feels like she should, because all those other emotions—particularly Sadness—are kinda *bad*. She doesn't even know who let them into Riley's brain in the first place. Isn't it better to be joyful all the time? Riley's parents initially seem to take that tack too. When the family moves to a new city in a new state, Riley's mom asks her daughter to put on a brave face, to *be happy*, for her father's sake.

But the film beautifully unpacks why even sadness is a critical emotion and how those emotions can mix and blend with each other to make our experiences all the richer, all the more powerful. It also introduced me to Riley's Islands of Personality—where her passions and priorities are delightfully illustrated.

When I left my screening of *Inside Out*, I thought about my own Islands of Personality and what they would look like. More importantly, I thought about how *Inside Out*—through those islands and its emotional avatars—could give parents like me new ways to talk with my kids about what they're thinking and feeling. I'm sure that *Inside Out* inspired many a conversation between parent and child—including some that are yet to happen.

Sure, the movie's obvious and nearly immediate takeaway value for parents is a rarity in the movie world. We don't have to be too movie savvy to understand that the Pixar film had a lot of things on its cinematic mind and a desire to pass those things onto its audience. Director Pete Docter enlisted the help of experts to make sure *Inside Out* was psychologically sound. And it worked.

But while the film's deliberateness was unusual, its role as a conversation catalyst is hardly unique. All sorts of films (and television shows and books and even video games) give us a chance to dig into big questions and important conversations with our kids. Many superhero movies can give you an opportunity to talk to your teens about heroism and sacrifice and doing the right thing even when it's hard. Sci-fi films can probe complex but important topics, ranging from the use and abuse of technology in our lives to what, exactly, life itself is. Many kids' movies are incredibly sophisticated, filled with messages about family and friendship and plenty of other topics too.

Name any halfway decent movie, and chances are good that you'll find at least one conversation just begging to be had, lurking in the wings as the credits roll. *Great* bits of entertainment might prompt a dozen or more conversations.

While sometimes those conversations can be difficult, they can still be important. For instance: The first time I really considered the concept of death wasn't at a funeral but during a nearly forgotten G-rated movie.

Where the Lilies Bloom is about a group of sharecropping kids in North Carolina who, after their father dies, pretty much raise themselves. Worried that the family will be split up if anyone finds out their dad is gone, they lie about his whereabouts to any adult who comes within earshot.

There's a lot more to it than that. But the only thing I really remember is the sickly, dying father. He went from weak to invalid to corpse to gone very quickly—and it sent me reeling.

Most viewers probably found *Where the Lilies Bloom* a sweet, innocent story of determination and resilience. For me, it was a horror story, plain and simple. I'd heard of people dying. I even knew of some people who died. But the finality of it—what I saw in the film—rocked my world.

Every scene after the father's death felt like a black hole to my five-year-old mind, a scene swirling around the dark absence of someone who should've been there and was never, ever coming back. And, of course, I thought of my own family. What would happen if *my* dad died? *My* mom? I didn't have any brothers and sisters to take care of me. What would *I* do?

I probably had some nightmares after that movie. I know that in the wake of it, my parents reassured me that they weren't going anywhere. And I think that made me feel better. But the fact that I still remember the feelings I had watching the movie—more, in fact, than the movie itself—drives home how influential that throwaway flick was in my childhood.

I don't think I'm alone. I think a lot of kids face death for the first time in movies, be it *Bambi* or *The Lion King* or any number of other films made for kids. In chapter 5, Adam talked about his own daughter's encounter with movie-based tragedy. Movies are often where the shadowed face of absence first takes off its cowl. While we as parents may be inclined to shield our children from these existential terrors (and, often, we should), we also must understand that we can't protect our kids permanently (as Adam also talked about).

Death is as much a part of life as life itself. Whether we tackle the subject at a grandmother's funeral or after King Mufasa's tumble off a cliff, it must be tackled sometime. In some ways, films give us an opportunity to deal with the subject proactively—to remind our children that death isn't the end; that life, even if we don't see it, can still go on. Pointing to Mufasa's image in the clouds later in *The Lion*

King can help reinforce that very critical point: The people we love never really leave us, even if we don't see them. Their laughter lurks in our minds, their voices in our hearts. And, God willing, we will one day see them again. We will run into their arms and laugh together.

Entertainment Can Help Us Develop Empathy

I am a white evangelical. I grew up and still live in Colorado Springs, where less than 7 percent of the population is black. Racial tension? When almost everyone you run into looks like you, it feels like a nonissue. I didn't get why race was such a big deal as a kid.

Then I went to a predominantly black church. And I got just a tiny taste of what being part of a minority feels like.

I went because my dad was invited to speak there. Everyone was as nice as they could be to us, but the music was far more robust than we Presbyterians were used to. The call-and-response style of preaching ("Amen!" "Hallelujah!" "That's right, brother!") would've been literally unheard of in the pews I grew up in. I was about fourteen at the time, an age when most of us long to fit in. It's a season where looking or acting different—from wearing pants that are too short or the wrong sort of shoes—makes you feel like an outcast. And here I was with my family, the only pale faces in a sea of dark ones.

I felt so different. So *other*. As energizing as the service was and as wonderful as the people were, I felt uneasy. Like I didn't belong.

But on the way home, I had a sudden epiphany that

I should've had years earlier: *That must be what my black friends feel like every single day.*

I didn't understand then that my black friends likely dealt with far, far worse experiences on a weekly basis. I had no context, no sense of history. But as a movie reviewer, I've had the ability and, I think, the honor to understand that context and history incrementally better through the movies I've seen.

Till, from 2022, is just one such example. The movie focuses on Mamie Till-Mobley, mother of fourteen-year-old Emmett Till, who was beaten and lynched in 1955 for whistling at a white woman. Mamie becomes an advocate for civil rights in the midst of her grief, insisting on holding an open-casket funeral for her horribly disfigured boy.

"Let the people see what they did to my boy," she says.[3]

Through movies and other media, the whole world has an opportunity to enter into different cultures, different experiences. They can help us see what we'd otherwise not have opportunity to. Sometimes these sorts of films and TV shows are not what you'd call entertainment. You don't go to a movie like *Till* for its laughs or thrills. You see it to be moved. To be challenged. And for those of us who've never experienced one iota of racism, you go to step into a pair of unfamiliar shoes. By walking in those shoes for even a couple of hours, you might find your outlook and understanding in a slightly different place than before.

In the hands of the amazing Danielle Deadwyler, Mamie becomes a lens through which to see the United States as it felt to many in 1955. We see through her the indescribable challenges of growing up black in the rural South—and the fear she feels sending her boy for what he sees as an innocent vacation. We see, of course, the shocking horrors of racism, from the lynching itself to the foregone conclusion that Emmett's killers will be acquitted. But the movie shows that racism extends into enclaves, and people, where you'd not readily expect it: the security guard who suggests Mamie look for shoes down in a department-store basement, for instance, or her own attorneys, who neglect to shake her hand.

We've seen dozens of incredibly moving, awards-caliber films about race hit the theaters in recent years—so much so that you could argue we're in the midst of a golden age of such cinematic stories. I feel fortunate to have had the opportunity to see and review so many of these films. Good stories can change you. And I feel that movies such as *Till* have changed me.

Movies can help us understand people who don't look like us or act like us. They can take us to unfamiliar parts of the world and give us a hint as to what it's like to survive there. They can bring us experiences we'd never be able to access otherwise (and perhaps never want to). *Beautiful Boy*, a 2018 film starring Steve Carell and Timothée Chalamet, showed us what drug addiction looks like through the eyes of an addict's father. *Nomadland* (2020) allows us to cross the country with a woman who lives out of her van—and wouldn't want it any other way. *The Florida Project* (2017) introduces us to people living at the very edge of existence next door to Disney World, "the happiest place on earth."

These are not always easy movies to watch. Indeed, all the

films I just mentioned are rated R and have content issues that adults and families need to consider carefully before watching. But these stories, when we're prepared and our children are mature enough to engage with them, can be valuable. And if you want to encourage a little cross-cultural empathy and understanding in your kids, you can find age-appropriate films that fit the bill—even if they, too, can be difficult and almost demand discussion afterward. The PG-13–rated *Till* is one such film, and there are plenty more.

Entertainment Can Help Us Understand the Art of Storytelling

Read the Bible cold, and it can be pretty confusing. It's not like a nice coherent novel that you can read from cover to cover with a limited cast of characters and a seamless, easy-to-follow plot.

Oh, certainly, there's an overarching story: It tells of God's unquenchable love for us, how we betrayed that love (again and again), and how God found a way to bridge that unbridgeable rift via His Son. But in the telling of that story, the Bible's form and function jump around a ton: Sometimes it's history; sometimes it's poetry; sometimes it's nice little proverbs, suitable for tweeting or pinning on your refrigerator. It can jump from small, gritty stories of poor widows and shepherds to the surreal fever-dream visions of prophets. Stories can shrink to the size of a womb and grow to the size of the cosmos. From end to end, the Bible is filled with loads of characters with weird names, often doing weird things that no one's done for hundreds, even thousands, of years.

And don't even get me started on Revelation.

To truly understand the Bible requires more than just sifting through its eight hundred thousand words (give or take). It requires an understanding of the culture it was written in, the authors who wrote it, the audiences they were writing for, and the forms they were using. The Bible is, on myriad levels, a work of art. You can't fully understand or even begin to truly appreciate it without at least some aesthetic understanding of what it's up to. Otherwise, most of us would've shut the book and never picked it up again after about the fourth *begat*.

The Bible doesn't just spoon-feed us; it demands something of us, just as God does. The Bible asks us to think, to feel, to give even the most simple-seeming passage our thought, our prayer, and our devotion. And as we do that, the Good Book constantly rewards us with more insights, more beauty, more understanding of God's love and character. It never changes, and yet our depth of understanding of it is always changing—because we do. And even if we've been reading the Bible for eighty years, we're still discovering new beauties within its pages.

Movies can be, at their best and in their own superficial way, a little like that. They reward attention. They reward thought. Sometimes they can become true art. The literal artistry of, say, the original *Pinocchio*, can't be denied. The artistic power of a *Schindler's List* or the raw cinematic beauty of *Lawrence of Arabia* is fairly obvious.

I think even schlocky, throwaway movies can have elements of storytelling "art" in them: The moviemakers have a story they want to tell. But the vocabulary and techniques they use are different from what you'd find in, say, a novel. Instead of words, they have pictures. Instead of punctuation, they have cuts and camera angles. Understanding that visual vocabulary, and how it's being used, can help us better understand the story. And understanding the "art" behind the story of movie can also help us pay attention to a story's cinematic "tricks"—how it encourages you to feel a certain way, or to sympathize with certain characters, or to be fooled into jumping at a jump scare.

Knowing something about what moviemakers are trying to do can, in other words, make good, worthy stories better. It can help protect you against the charms of unworthy ones. And learning some of these techniques, as well as slowly, gently helping your children understand them, too, can help you be all the more able to navigate the entertainment-soaked world we live in—and guard against its negative influences.

Indeed, movies made for kids—animated movies—are often the best forums for exploring what filmmakers try to do with shape and color, music, and even symbolism. The makers of animated movies, after all, aren't tied to how actors look or how the setting feels. They can make it up, and everything they design can help feed the story they're trying to tell and the points they're trying to make.

For me, another Pixar movie, *Up*,[4] offers a terrific example of how understanding the "art" of a particular movie can enrich the story it's trying to tell. In this case, the art we're talking about is quite literal.

Carl Fredricksen is *Up*'s grumpy hero. He's a grounded, no-nonsense individual who's not prone to flights of fancy.

We know this by how he looks: His entire character is shaped around what appear to be squat blocks. His chin is square. His glasses are square. Everything about him is solid and angled. Contrast that with Ellie, his longtime wife. Her face is round. Her angles are soft. Taken together, they're a study in complementary opposites. Visually, we can see how their relationship works. Carl keeps the couple grounded. Ellie is the vibrant, buoyant adventurer who can lift Carl's spirit. Almost, when you think about it, like a *balloon*.

When Ellie dies, Carl remains in the house they shared together. The house, like Carl, is all squares and angles—solidly rooted to the ground. He, and it, even refuse to move for a massive construction project. But when it seems there's no way to halt the project—when the house is doomed and Carl's stolid, staid way of life is threatened—Carl decides to honor a promise he made to Ellie. He will travel to Paradise Falls in her honor. It's so fitting that he uses *balloons* to lift the house off the ground: The symbolism in play here is potent.

The film is filled with such visual hints: It's no accident that Russell, a young "Wilderness Explorer" who accidentally gets swept away with the house, is pretty rotund and balloon-like himself.

But, of course, live-action movies lean on plenty of similar storytelling techniques too. And almost every movie at least tries to use visual and audible queues—often subconsciously—to better tell the story it's trying to tell.

In the original *Wizard of Oz*, remember how Dorothy steps out of black-and-white Kansas farmland into a Technicolor wonderland? Cinematographers often do the same sort of thing (only in a far more subtle way), turning the landscape bluer or more monochrome to give the scene a bleaker feel, or more warm and rich to emphasize wonder and happiness. Directors will fill houses with odd angles to make you feel uneasy. Or they'll film characters from below to make you feel threatened.

The makers might add the sound of a ticking clock in the background to make a house feel lonely and empty or to suggest a sense of chronological urgency. But, of course, so much depends on context.

Pinocchio and season 4 of *Stranger Things* both prominently feature clocks, but their presence tells us very different things. In *Pinocchio*, Geppetto's colorful cuckoo clocks tell us a great deal about their maker—not just about his skill but also about his whimsy and humor. When he celebrates, Geppetto sets the clocks all going at once—a delightful, joyous cacophony of music and movement.

There's *nothing* whimsical about the grandfather clock in *Stranger Things*. But it, too, says a great deal about its owner: the near-demonic soul eater known as Vecna. The deep-voiced clock is a dark, huge, inescapable presence, looming in hallways and roads and nightmarish landscapes, counting the hours and minutes till the demise of Vecna's next victim. It lurks in the shadows like a monster—methodical and irresistible and relentless, like time itself.

If the clocks in *Pinocchio* are designed to encourage joy and laughter with each passing hour—to recall that time is a *gift*—Vecna's clock tells us that time, for the show's characters, and perhaps for us, too, is running out.

Most good stories are meant to be understood on different levels. You can think of them as, say, a mountain—part of the glorious story that God is telling us. You can take a walk through the forest and enjoy the experience. But take the time to engage all your senses—the scent of the ponderosas, the sound of the woodpeckers, the glory of the sky stretching out above you—and it deepens your appreciation. Sit down on a rock and study the moss on a tree trunk (almost always on the north side) or the shredded pine cones on the ground (ground squirrels have been busy), and they'll add to the story. Each pine needle, each critter scurrying just out of sight deepens the story and reminds you of its Teller.

The stories we tell will never match the stories of God, of course. But they can be rich and wonderful in their own way. And the more we understand and grapple with the visual stories we engage with—not just walk through them but *think* about them—the richer those stories will feel.

That word, *think*, is an inescapable part of the process. We can't set aside our brains. We shouldn't. We must sift our stories carefully. And the more we understand their language, the more effective our sifters can be.

Entertainment Can Help Us Connect to God

Maybe this feels obvious. Of the hundreds of movies released each year, a dozen or more are explicitly Christian films—movies made by Christians for, predominantly, Christian audiences. I've met many a believer who had given up on Hollywood and was lured back to the movies by *Fireproof* or *God's Not Dead* or *I Can Only Imagine*. For many, these movies can be deeply inspiring, encouraging, and edifying—as good as or better than any cinematic blockbuster or Oscar-winning film out there. Ask my father about his favorite movies, and he'll mention a slew of Christian ones. But when I tried to get him to watch *The Lord of the Rings* movies, he fell asleep during every one.

I certainly like a lot of Christian movies too. But ask me which movies make me think about God and faith, I might just say . . . *The Lord of the Rings* series.

Or I could point to *Roma*, a Netflix film that should've won the Best Picture award in 2019. Its humble house-keeper hero reminds me of the selfless daily sacrifice we're supposed to embrace. Or I might recall *Room*, the 2015 film that earned Brie Larson an Oscar. Though its subject matter is incredibly difficult (Larson plays a woman who was kidnapped and repeatedly raped by her captor, but that horrific abuse also gave her a son she dearly loved), I hear Christian echoes everywhere in this R-rated movie.

I love finding God in unexpected places—including, and perhaps especially, in movies. Maybe that's because of the way I process faith.

For some, including my dad, talking with God can seem as easy and as tangible as chatting with the neighbor next door. But for me, God has often felt . . . distant. I know He's with me, but I don't usually feel His presence. And when I do, it can feel overwhelming, as if I were Dorothy stepping out of Kansas into Oz.

For me, faith isn't often a feeling. It's a *choice*, and some days it's a difficult choice. Just like love. Just like submission.

Rarely do I chat with God as if He lives next door. Rather, He's across the mountains, hidden by peaks and valleys. It's only by following His cairns, painstakingly placed and sometimes difficult to find, that I reach Him. So when I see God so obviously on-screen, so clearly in story, it feels, perhaps, too easy. To see such a nice, pat resolution after a mere ninety minutes feels foreign to my understanding.

Maybe I'm like the guy who feels that riding a train up Pikes Peak is just too easy. If I'm going to get there, I need to hike it.

I'd imagine that Christians land all along a spectrum of faith. For some, the Christian walk is as easy as breathing. For others, it's a process, filled with seasons of knowing and doubt, times of song and silence. I suspect that God made us so—in order that we can be uniquely equipped to relate to both Him and others in a multitude of ways. Is it any surprise that different sorts of movies would connect with us too?

Certainly, if you and your kids connect powerfully with the Christian movies out there, your job is much easier. You can pick out characters you can relate to. You can pick out the messages that move you. Some movies and television shows (such as *The Chosen*) even come with ready-made devotionals and study guides that can help you grow in your faith and guide your family through questions and verses and interesting discussion points.

For those who want to find echoes of faith—find God's fingerprints—in less obvious movies, it can be a little trickier. *Plugged In* sometimes dives a little deeper into a given movie to explore its spiritual depth, which can help a bit. But oftentimes, it's up to you.

So as you watch films that aren't explicitly Christian, I'd encourage you to look for certain elements and ask certain questions. For instance: *When do characters act in line with what Scripture would have us do? When do they not? Do snippets of dialogue seem to echo or even quote Scripture?* Look for moments that seem to do so, even if they're only dim reflections of important moments in the Bible. For example, many characters go through symbolic "baptisms," where they're submerged in water and find themselves *new* somehow on the other side. It's not typically a sign they've become Christians, but movies and TV shows often use the language of Christianity to suggest that one life has died and another has been born. Moments like these—when you know about them and can point them out—might just encourage you to think about your own faith and talk about faith with others.

Yes, movies, television, and other entertainment mediums are extraordinarily powerful. They can be powerful enough to isolate us, warp us, and even lead us away from the Creator. We've hopefully shown you that in this book and given you tools to help guard yourself and your children from the negative influences that sneak through your screens.

But those screens don't just pump filth into our living rooms. They don't just pour putrescence into our minds. They can be, like that original message on Samuel Morse's telegraph line, full of purpose and portent. They can connect us to those we love. They can draw us closer to God. They can help us feel empathy and compassion for people we've never met. And sometimes, when we watch a powerful movie, they can even make us mindful of what, indeed, "God hath wrought."

Writing Our Own Stories

Paul Asay

"IN THE BEGINNING WAS THE WORD."

So begins John's Gospel. It's a conscious echo of Genesis; a recognition of the primacy of Scripture; a beautiful acknowledgment that before all *this*—our mountains, our trees, ourselves—there was a knowing of right, of good, of justice, of grace.

But it is, again, a nod to the importance of story in our worlds and our lives. We make our stories, and we are in turn made by them.

In this book, I hope we've conveyed to you why our own cultural stories—be they on sixty-foot-high screens or six-inch phones, written on pulpwood pages or scrawled digitally across the internet—are so important. I hope we've illustrated what makes them great or dangerous and how we can protect ourselves and our families from the stories (and the content therein) not worth our time.

But ultimately, all the stories we've talked about—in movies or television, in video games or social media—are important only because they impact your own story and the collective story of your family.

We're all cowriting our own stories, after all, and each and every one of our lives is worth telling on a three-story screen. In God's eyes, we all have the potential to be heroes. Each of us must overcome hardship and adversity, brave times that threaten to crush us. Our lives are dotted with people who can pull us up or push us down (and let's admit it, sometimes the same person can do a little of both). They're saturated with influences that can make us better or make us baser.

And God implores us, always, *Choose better.*

It's a cliché that our choices make us who we are, but it's true. Every moment we spend on this earth we choose to spend a certain way. And that makes our entertainment and social media choices all the more important. Do we choose to spend an hour with our kids or scrolling through TikTok? Do we choose to spend an evening finishing homework or finishing a game level? The time we spend with entertainment isn't necessarily wasted time . . . but it can be. The times I've spent playing *Mario Kart* with my kids, I'll treasure forever. The time I've spent watching throwaway shows, I'll never get back.

Choose better, God tells us.

Time is the most precious commodity we have (another cliché that's nevertheless true). The world encourages us to spend it in so many ways. Our children are watching us, testing us, asking us to guide them. How do we spend this most treasured of resources? How do we spend our dwindling fortune of time?

We spend it together, that's how. We spend it in ways that bring joy to God and happiness to each other. We reject the isolating time killers and time wasters. We push away the things that separate us into different rooms and different screens. Instead, we come together. We gather to play a game. We gather to watch and laugh at a terrible sci-fi movie. We gather to read a book. To sing along, out of tune, to TobyMac. To see a movie.

Each day is precious. Each moment is special. Your kids are growing up, growing older, growing to follow God or to walk away from Him. And the hours they spend—and you spend—with entertainment tell them something. Teach them something.

Choose better, God says.

We're creatures of story, you and I. And because of God's grace and love, we have the ability to tell our own. What are we saying with our stories? What lessons are we teaching? How are we shaping our own sons and daughters as they begin to understand that they, too, have a story to tell? And how, exactly, are we incorporating the stories all around us? Are they making us better? Or are they making us worse?

Be mindful of the stories you watch, read, listen to, play.

They impact your own. They impact your children. They can be beautiful, powerful, inspirational, honoring. And they can be anything but. Very often, they can be both. Remember their importance. Understand their influence.

Choose better.

Notes

INTRODUCTION | THE POWER OF STORY
1. Madeleine L'Engle, *Walking on Water: Reflections on Faith and Art* (New York: North Point Press, 1995), 81.
2. C. S. Lewis, *The Horse and His Boy* (1982; New York: HarperCollins, 1994), 167.

CHAPTER ONE | REMOTE
1. Victoria Rideout and Michael B. Robb, *The Common Sense Census: Media Use by Tweens and Teens* (San Francisco: Common Sense Media, 2019), 3, https://www.commonsensemedia.org/sites/default/files/research/report/2019-census-8-to-18-full-report-updated.pdf.
2. Sheri Madigan et al., "Assessment of Changes in Child and Adolescent Screen Time during the COVID-19 Pandemic: A Systematic Review and Meta-analysis," *JAMA Pediatrics* 176, no. 12 (2022), https://jamanetwork.com/journals/jamapediatrics/fullarticle/2798256.
3. Craig T. Lee, "Screen Zombies: Average Person Will Spend 44 Years Looking at Digital Devices—and That's before COVID!," StudyFinds, December 26, 2020, https://studyfinds.org/screen-zombies-average-person-spends-44-years-looking-at-devices.

4. "Neutral Zone," StarTrek.com, accessed June 1, 2023, https://www.startrek .com/database_article/neutral-zone.

CHAPTER TWO | WE GET ONLY ONE BRAIN

1. Jamie Waters, "Constant Craving: How Digital Media Turned Us All into Dopamine Addicts," *Guardian*, August 22, 2021, https://www.theguardian .com/global/2021/aug/22/how-digital-media-turned-us-all-into-dopamine -addicts-and-what-we-can-do-to-break-the-cycle.
2. Peter Whybrow, quoted in Mary A. Fischer, "Manic Nation: Dr. Peter Whybrow Says We're Addicted to Stress," *Pacific Standard*, June 14, 2017, https://psmag.com/social-justice/manic-nation-dr-peter-whybrow-says -were-addicted-stress-42695.
3. Andrew Doan, quoted in Nicholas Kardaras, "It's 'Digital Heroin': How Screens Turn Kids into Psychotic Junkies," *New York Post*, August 27, 2016, https://nypost.com/2016/08/27/its-digital-heroin-how-screens-turn-kids -into-psychotic-junkies.
4. Wanjun Guo et al., "Associations of Internet Addiction Severity with Psychopathology, Serious Mental Illness, and Suicidality: Large-Sample Cross-Sectional Study," *Journal of Medical Internet Research* 22, no. 8 (August 2020), https://www.ncbi.nlm.nih.gov/pmc/articles/PMC7448182.
5. Guo, "Associations of Internet Addiction."
6. Nick Bilton, "Steve Jobs Was a Low-Tech Parent," *New York Times*, September 10, 2014, https://www.nytimes.com/2014/09/11/fashion/steve-jobs-apple -was-a-low-tech-parent.html.
7. Adam J. Krause, "The Sleep-Deprived Human Brain," *Nature Reviews Neuroscience* 18, no. 7 (July 2017): 404–18, https://www.ncbi.nlm.nih .gov/pmc/articles/PMC6143346; Eti Ben Simon, Raphael Vallat, Aubrey Rossi, and Matthew P. Walker, "Sleep Loss Leads to the Withdrawal of Human Helping across Individuals, Groups, and Large-Scale Societies," *PLOS Biology* 20, no. 8 (August 2022), https://journals.plos.org/plosbiology /article?id=10.1371/journal.pbio.3001733; Ziyi Peng, "Effect of Sleep Deprivation on the Working Memory–Related N2–P3 Components of the Event-Related Potential Waveform," *Frontiers in Neuroscience* 14 (May 2020), https://www.frontiersin.org/articles/10.3389/fnins.2020.00469/full; Jolanta Orzel-Gryglewska, "Consequences of Sleep Deprivation," *International Journal of Occupational Medicine and Environmental Health* 23, no. 1 (2010): 95–114, https://psycnet.apa.org/record/2010-13439-002; Muhammed Bishir, "Sleep Deprivation and Neurological Disorders," *BioMed Research International* (November 2020), https://www.hindawi .com/journals/bmri/2020/5764017; "Sufficient Sleep Associated with Life Satisfaction in Parents, New Study Finds," Health and Human Development, Penn State, September 21, 2022, https://www.psu.edu/news/health-and -human-development/story/sufficient-sleep-associated-life-satisfaction -parents-new-study.

8. Claire Holt, "How TikTok Is Ruining Your Attention Span," Medium.com, October 11, 2021, https://medium.com/@clairemholt/how-tiktok-is -ruining-your-attention-span-2beb9a1d5b72.

9. Renata Maria Silva Santos, "The Association between Screen Time and Attention in Children: A Systematic Review," *Developmental Neuropsychology* 47, no. 4 (July 2022): 175–92, https://pubmed.ncbi.nlm.nih.gov/35430923.

10. Aaron Chi, "A Brief History of Neuromarketing," Boonmind, February 24, 2022, https://www.boonmind.com/a-brief-history-of-neuromarketing.

11. Anika Hussen, "Neurocinematics: How Do You Feel When Watching a Film?," *NaturallyHealthy* (blog), October 9, 2018, https://wp.nyu.edu/naturallyhealth /2018/10/09/neurocinematics-how-do-you-feel-when-watching-a-film.

12. Survey conducted May 1–10, 2018, cited in "Americans' Moral Stance towards Pornography 2018," Statista, accessed June 2, 2023, https://www .statista.com/statistics/225972/americans-moral-stance-towards-pornography.

13. Richard Weissbourd, "Loneliness in America: How the Pandemic Has Deepened an Epidemic of Loneliness and What We Can Do about It," Making Caring Common Project, February 2021, https://mcc.gse.harvard .edu/reports/loneliness-in-america.

14. Everyday Health online survey conducted October 2017, published in *Special Report: State of Women's Wellness 2017* (Dallas: Research Now, 2017), 31, https://images.agoramedia.com/everydayhealth/gcms/Everyday-Health -State-of-Womens-Wellness-Survey-PDF.pdf.

15. Nicole Plumridge, "Communication: Online vs. Face-to-Face Interactions," Psychminds, April 13, 2020, https://psychminds.com/communication-online -vs-face-to-face-interactions.

16. "The Impact of Social Media on Teens' Mental Health," Health, University of Utah, January 20, 2023, https://healthcare.utah.edu/healthfeed/2023/01 /impact-of-social-media-teens-mental-health.

17. Nationwide survey conducted by Lake Research Partners, February–March, 2016, cited in "Dealing with Devices: The Parent-Teen Dynamic," Common Sense Media, accessed June 3, 2023, https://www.commonsensemedia .org/technology-addiction-concern-controversy-and-finding-balance -infographic.

18. Lyndsay Jerusha Mackay, "Impacts of Parental Technoference on Parent-Child Relationships and Child Health and Developmental Outcomes: A Scoping Review Protocol," *Systematic Reviews* 11, no. 45 (2022), https://systematicreviewsjournal.biomedcentral.com/articles /10.1186/s13643-022-01918-3#.

CHAPTER THREE | BELIEF

1. "How a Racist Film Helped the Ku Klux Klan Grow for Generations," *Economist*, March 27, 2021, https://www.economist.com/graphic-detail/2021 /03/27/how-a-racist-film-helped-the-ku-klux-klan-grow-for-generations.

2. Data cited in Katie O'Toole, "The Power of Cinema: 10 Films That Changed

the World," Raindance, January 29, 2019, https://raindance.org/the-power
-of-cinema-10-films-that-changed-the-world.

3. Roger Ebert, quoted in Claire Mulkerin, "Movies That Actually Changed
the World," Looper, July 19, 2021, https://www.looper.com/149503/movies
-that-actually-changed-the-world.

4. Bobby, in *Bros*, directed by Nicholas Stoller (Universal City, CA: Universal
Pictures, 2022).

5. *Spider-Man: Far from Home*, directed by John Watts (Culver City, CA:
Columbia Pictures, 2019).

6. Mysterio, in *Spider-Man: Far from Home*.

7. A. W. Tozer, *The Knowledge of the Holy* (New York: HarperOne, 1978), 1.

8. C. S. Lewis, *The Weight of Glory and Other Addresses* (New York: Macmillan,
1949), 10.

9. Jeffrey M. Jones, "U.S. Church Membership Falls below Majority for First
Time," Gallup.com, March 29, 2021, https://news.gallup.com/poll/341963
/church-membership-falls-below-majority-first-time.aspx.

10. Survey conducted April 25–June 4, 2017, cited in Michael Lipka and Claire
Gecewicz, "More Americans Now Say They're Spiritual but Not Religious,"
Pew Research Center, September 6, 2017, https://www.pewresearch.org/short
-reads/2017/09/06/more-americans-now-say-theyre-spiritual-but-not
-religious.

11. Survey conducted March 29–April 14, 2019, cited in Jeff Diamant and
Elizabeth Podrebarac Sciupac, "10 Key Findings about the Religious Lives of
U.S. Teens and Their Parents," Pew Research Center, September 10, 2020,
https://www.pewresearch.org/fact-tank/2020/09/10/10-key-findings-about
-the-religious-lives-of-u-s-teens-and-their-parents.

12. Religious Landscape Study, conducted June 4–September 30, 2014, cited
in Carlyle Murphy, "Most U.S. Christian Groups Grow More Accepting of
Homosexuality," Pew Research Center, December 18, 2015, https://www
.pewresearch.org/short-reads/2015/12/18/most-u-s-christian-groups-grow
-more-accepting-of-homosexuality.

13. Spencer Perry, "Neil Gaiman Reveals His Contributions to Alan Moore's
Watchmen Script," ComicBook.com, August 27, 2022, https://comicbook
.com/dc/news/neil-gaiman-contributions-alan-moore-watchmen-script.

14. *Thor*, directed by Kenneth Branagh (Hollywood: Paramount Pictures, 2011).

15. *The Avengers*, directed by Joss Whedon (Hollywood: Paramount Pictures,
2012).

16. Scott Feinberg, "Martin Scorsese Defends 'The Wolf of Wall Street': 'The
Devil Comes with a Smile' (Q&A)," *Hollywood Reporter*, December 31,
2013, https://www.hollywoodreporter.com/news/general-news/martin
-scorsese-defends-wolf-wall-667851.

17. *La La Land*, directed by Damien Chazelle (Santa Monica, CA: Summit
Entertainment, 2016).

18. *No Country for Old Men*, directed by Ethan Coen and Joel Coen (Los Angeles: Paramount Vantage, 2007).
19. Film quotations in this section from *The Dark Knight*, directed by Christopher Nolan (Burbank, CA: Warner Brothers, 2008).
20. *Groundhog Day*, directed by Harold Ramis (Culver City, CA: Columbia Pictures, 1993).
21. Batman and the Joker, in *The Dark Knight*.
22. J. R. R. Tolkien, *The Fellowship of the Ring*, 2nd ed., The Lord of the Rings (Boston: Houghton Mifflin, 1965), 65.
23. Andrew Bloom, "The Dark Knight and the Dangerous Legacy of the Charismatic Villain," *Consequence*, July 19, 2018, https://consequence .net/2018/07/the-dark-knight-and-the-dangerous-legacy-of-the-charismatic -villain.
24. Ryan Parker, "Aurora Shooting Victims Voice Fears over 'Joker' in Letter to Warner Bros.," *Hollywood Reporter*, September 24, 2019, https://www .hollywoodreporter.com/news/general-news/aurora-shooting-victims-voice -concerns-joker-emotional-letter-warner-bros-1241599.

CHAPTER FOUR | CHRIST ON YOUR COUCH

1. Athenagoras, *A Plea for the Christians*, trans. B. P. Pratten (n.p.: Logos Library), ch. 35, http://logoslibrary.org/athenagoras/plea/35.html.
2. Trace William Cowen, "HBO Is Reportedly Forcing Pornhub to Remove 'Game of Thrones' Content," Complex.com, June 1, 2016, https://www .complex.com/pop-culture/2016/06/hbo-forcing-pornhub-remove-game-of- thrones-content; Ben Kayser, "*Game of Thrones* Is So Graphic, Porn Websites Are Stealing the Content," MOVIEGUIDE, accessed June 5, 2023, https://www.movieguide.org/news-articles/games-thrones-graphic-websites -stealing-content.html.
3. Olivia Rodrigo, quoted in Dina Sartore-Bodo and Russ Weakland, "Olivia Rodrigo's Proud Her 'High School Musical' Series Character Has 2 Moms: It's 'Important' for Kids to See," Hollywood Life.com, November 15, 2019, https://hollywoodlife.com/2019/11/15/olivia-rodrigo-high-school-musical -interview-lesbian-moms. Emphasis added.

CHAPTER FIVE | THE GAME PLAN

1. Tibi Puiu, "Your Smartphone Is Millions of Times More Powerful than the Apollo 11 Guidance Computers," ZME Science, May 11, 2023, https://www .zmescience.com/science/news-science/smartphone-power-compared-to -apollo-432.
2. Daniel P. Huerta, *7 Traits of Effective Parenting* (Colorado Springs: Focus on the Family, 2020), 96.
3. Annie Dillard, *The Writing Life* (New York: HarperPerennial, 1990), 32.
4. American Academy of Child and Adolescent Psychiatry, "Screen Time and

Children," February 2020, https://www.aacap.org/AACAP/Families_and
_Youth/Facts_for_Families/FFF-Guide/Children-And-Watching-TV
-054.aspx.

5. Victoria Rideout et al., *The Common Sense Census: Media Use by Tweens
and Teens* (San Francisco: Common Sense Media, 2021), 3, https://www
.commonsensemedia.org/sites/default/files/research/report/8-18-census
-integrated-report-final-web_0.pdf.

CHAPTER SIX | WHEN THINGS GO WRONG

1. Diana Baumrind, cited in Francyne Zeltser, "A Psychologist Shares the
4 Styles of Parenting—and the Type That Researchers Say Is the Most
Successful," CNBC Make It, July 1, 2021, https://www.cnbc.com/2021
/06/29/child-psychologist-explains-4-types-of-parenting-and-how-to-tell
-which-is-right-for-you.html.

CHAPTER SEVEN | PLAYING THE LONG GAME

1. Robert K. Johnston, *Reel Spirituality: Theology and Film in Dialogue* (Grand
Rapids: Baker Academic, 2006).

2. "History of Ratings," FilmRatings.com, accessed June 6, 2023, https://www
.filmratings.com/History.

CHAPTER EIGHT | SCREENING THOSE SCREENS

1. Jean-Luc Godard, quoted in "'Cinema Is the Most Beautiful Fraud': 10
Profound Sayings of Jean-Luc Godard," *Economic Times*, September 13, 2022,
https://economictimes.indiatimes.com/news/new-updates/cinema-is-the
-most-beautiful-fraud-10-profound-sayings-of-jean-luc-godard/articleshow
/94181711.cms.

2. Nathalia Aryani, review of *Avatar: The Way of Water*, directed by James
Cameron, *MovieMaven* (blog), December 25, 2022, https://www
.rottentomatoes.com/critics/nathalia-aryani/movies.

3. *Avatar: The Way of Water*, directed by James Cameron (Los Angeles: 20th
Century Studios, 2022).

4. James Cameron, quoted in Richard Trenholm, "James Cameron Q&A:
'Avatar' Reminds Us of the Beauty of Nature under Threat," CNET,
December 14, 2022, https://www.cnet.com/culture/entertainment/james
-cameron-q-a-avatar-way-of-water-reminds-us-of-the-beauty-of-nature
-under-threat.

5. Selome Hailu, "Netflix Top 10: 'Stranger Things 4' Becomes Second Title
Ever to Cross 1 Billion Hours Viewed," *Variety*, July 5, 2022, https://variety
.com/2022/tv/news/netflix-top-10-stranger-things-season-4-volume-2-billion
-hours-1235309293.

6. Abigail Abrams, "361,000 People Binge-Watched All of Stranger Things in a
Day," *Time*, November 2, 2017, https://time.com/5008471/stranger-things-2
-neilsen-ratings-binge.

7. James Hibberd, "'Breaking Bad' Series Finale Ratings Smash All Records," *Entertainment Weekly*, September 30, 2013, https://ew.com/article/2013 /09/30/breaking-bad-series-finale-ratings.

8. Frank Pallotta, "'Game of Thrones' Ended with a Thud. But 'House of the Dragon' Has Caught Fire," CNN Business, October 9, 2022, https://www .cnn.com/2022/10/09/media/house-of-the-dragon-viewership.

9. Michael Schneider, "100 Most-Watched TV Shows of 2019–20: Winners and Losers," *Variety*, May 21, 2020, https://variety.com/2020/tv/news/most -popular-tv-shows-highest-rated-2019-2020-season-masked-singer-last-dance -1234612885.

10. Jeremy Dick, "Game of Thrones Remains the Most Pirated TV Series in 2022," MovieWeb.com, July 15, 2022, https://movieweb.com/game-of -thrones-most-pirated-2022.

11. Eliza Thompson, "'Game of Thrones' and 'House of the Dragon' Controversies through the Years: Incest, 'Sexposition,' and More," *US Weekly*, October 23, 2022, https://www.usmagazine.com/entertainment/pictures /game-of-thrones-controversies-over-the-years-sexposition.

12. Tracy Brown, "Commentary: 'She-Ra' Rewrote the Script for TV's Queer Love Stories. Here's Why It Matters," *Los Angeles Times*, May 18, 2020, https://www.latimes.com/entertainment-arts/tv/story/2020-05-18/netflix -she-ra-series-finale-queer-love-wins.

13. Whitesnake, "Here I Go Again," lyrics by Bernie Marsden and David Coverdale, *Saints and Sinners* (album), copyright 1982, Sony/ATV Music.

14. Mark Joseph Stern, "Neural Nostalgia: Why Do We Love the Music We Heard as Teenagers?," *Slate*, August 12, 2014, https://slate.com/technology /2014/08/musical-nostalgia-the-psychology-and-neuroscience-for-song -preference-and-the-reminiscence-bump.html.

15. C. S. Lewis, *The Last Battle* (New York: Collier Books, 1970), 120.

16. Erich Maria Remarque, *All Quiet on the Western Front*, ed. Helmuth Kiesel, trans. A. W. Wheen (New York: Continuum, 2004), 7.

17. Kabir L., "Video Game Addiction: The Comprehensive Guide," Healthy Gamer, January 26, 2021, https://www.healthygamer.gg/blog/video-game -addiction.

18. Ewa Miedzobrodzka et al., "Is It Painful? Playing Violent Video Games Affects Brain Responses to Painful Pictures: An Event-Related Potential Study," *Psychology of Popular Media* 11, no. 1 (2022): 13–23, cited in Beth Ellwood, "People Who Frequently Play Violent Video Games Like Call of Duty Show Neural Desensitization to Painful Images, according to Study," PsyPost, January 28, 2022, https://www.psypost.org/2022/01/people-who -frequently-play-call-of-duty-show-neural-desensitization-to-painful-images -according-to-study-62264.

19. American Academy of Pediatrics recommendations on gaming limits, cited in Nancy M. Petry, "Healthy Limits on Video Games: How to Prevent (or

Overcome) Problems with Gaming," Child Mind Institute, accessed January 17, 2023, https://childmind.org/article/healthy-limits-on-video-games.

20. *Charlie the Unicorn*, FilmCow (YouTube), posted January 10, 2008, https://www.youtube.com/watch?v=CsGYh8AacgY.

21. Patrick van Kessel, Skye Toor, and Aaron Smith, "A Week in the Life of Popular YouTube Channels," Pew Research Center, July 25, 2019, https://www.pewresearch.org/internet/2019/07/25/a-week-in-the-life -of-popular-youtube-channels.

22. "Hours of Video Uploaded to YouTube Every Minute 2007–2022," February 2022, https://www.statista.com/statistics/259477/hours-of-video-uploaded -to-youtube-every-minute.

23. Van Kessel, "Popular YouTube Channels."

24. "About YouTube," YouTube.com, accessed June 7, 2023, https://about .youtube.

25. Survey conducted April 14–May 4, 2022, cited in Emily A. Vogels, Risa Gelles-Watnick, and Navid Massarat, "Teens, Social Media, and Technology," Pew Research Center, August 10, 2022, https://www.pewresearch.org/internet /2022/08/10/teens-social-media-and-technology-2022.

26. Victoria Rideout et al., *The Common Sense Census: Media Use by Tweens and Teens* (San Francisco: Common Sense Media, 2021), 4, https://www .commonsensemedia.org/sites/default/files/research/report/8-18-census -integrated-report-final-web_0.pdf.

27. Celie O'Neil-Hart and Howard Blumenstein, "Why YouTube Stars Are More Influential Than Traditional Celebrities," Think with Google, July 2016, https://www.thinkwithgoogle.com/marketing-strategies/video/youtube -stars-influence.

28. *Children and Parents: Media Use and Attitudes Report 2022* (London: Ofcom, 2022), 57, https://www.ofcom.org.uk/__data/assets/pdf_file/0024/234609 /childrens-media-use-and-attitudes-report-2022.pdf.

29. Amanda N. Tolbert and Kristin L. Drogos, "Tweens' Wishful Identification and Parasocial Relationships with YouTubers," *Frontiers in Psychology* 10 (2019), https://www.frontiersin.org/articles/10.3389/fpsyg.2019.02781/full.

CHAPTER NINE | THE TECHNOLOGY CURVE

1. Survey conducted March 2–15, 2020, cited in Brooke Auxier et al., "Parenting Children in the Age of Screens," Pew Research Center, July 28, 2020, https://www.pewresearch.org/internet/2020/07/28/parenting-children -in-the-age-of-screens.

2. Steven Spielberg, quoted on Goodreads, accessed June 8, 2023, https://www .goodreads.com/quotes/706707-technology-can-be-our-best-friend-and -technology-can-also.

3. Pew survey conducted March 7–April 10, 2018, cited in Katherine Schaeffer, "Most U.S. Teens Who Use Cellphones Do It to Pass Time, Connect with

Others, Learn New Things," Pew Research Center, August 23, 2019, https://www.pewresearch.org/short-reads/2019/08/23/most-u-s-teens-who -use-cellphones-do-it-to-pass-time-connect-with-others-learn-new-things.

4. Ramin Mojtabai, Mark Ofson, and Beth Han, "National Trends in the Prevalence and Treatment of Depression in Adolescents and Young Adults," *Pediatrics* 138, no. 6 (2016), cited in Leah Shafer, "Social Media and Teen Anxiety," *Usable Knowledge*, December 15, 2017, https://www.gse.harvard .edu/news/uk/17/12/social-media-and-teen-anxiety.

5. "Teens and Social Media Use: What's the Impact?," Tween and Teen Health, Mayo Clinic, accessed June 8, 2023, https://www.mayoclinic.org/healthy -lifestyle/tween-and-teen-health/in-depth/teens-and-social-media-use/art -20474437.

6. "The Phenomenon of 'Sexting' and Its Risks to Youth," National Center on Sexual Exploitation, March 9, 2021, https://endsexualexploitation .org/articles/the-phenomenon-of-sexting-and-its-risks-to-youth.

7. Pew survey conducted April 14–May 4, 2022, cited in Emily A. Vogels, Risa Gelles-Watnick, and Navid Massarat, "Teens, Social Media, and Technology," Pew Research Center, August 10, 2022, https://www.pewresearch.org/internet /2022/08/10/teens-social-media-and-technology-2022; Survey of thirteen- to seventeen-year-olds conducted September 2022, cited in Michael B. Robb and Supreet Mann, *Teens and Pornography* (San Francisco: Common Sense, 2023), 5, https://www.commonsensemedia.org/sites/default/files/research /report/2022-teens-and-pornography-final-web.pdf.

8. Hilary Anderson, "Social Media Apps Are 'Deliberately' Addictive to Users," BBC News, July 4, 2018, https://www.bbc.com/news/technology -44640959.

9. Vogels, "Teens, Social Media, and Technology."

10. Adam Holz, "Of Algorithms, Eating Disorders, and Social Media," PluggedIn.com, January 12, 2022, https://www.pluggedin.com/blog/of -algorithms-eating-disorders-and-social-media.

11. Quispe López, "6 Tech Executives Who Raise Their Kids Tech-Free or Seriously Limit Their Screen Time," *Insider*, March 5, 2020, https://www .businessinsider.com/tech-execs-screen-time-children-bill-gates-steve-jobs -2019-9.

12. Valerie Carson et al., "Physical Activity and Sedentary Behavior across Three Time-Points and Associations with Social Skills in Early Childhood," *BMC Public Health* 19, no. 27 (2019), https://bmcpublichealth.biomedcentral. com/articles/10.1186/s12889-018-6381-x.

13. "We Did All the Research on Screen Time and Here's What We Found," Lovevery, accessed June 8, 2023, https://lovevery.com/community/blog /child-development/we-did-all-the-research-on-screen-time-and-heres-what -we-found.

14. Associated Press, "World Health Organization Says If Your Baby Is Younger Than 1 Year Old, They Should Spend No Time in Front of Your

Smartphone," *Insider*, April 24, 2019, https://www.insider.com/world
-health-organization-releases-new-screen-time-guidance-for-babies-2019-4
?_gl=1*1ghp1r7*_ga*MTE0MDE5NTk5Ny4xNjk1Mzk1MDQ0*_ga_E21
CV80ZCZ*MTY5NTM5NTA0My4xLjEuMTY5NTM5NTA0OS41NC4
wLjA.

15. Jonathan McKee, "At What Age Should I Let My Kid Have a Phone?,"
Jonathan McKee (blog), May 3, 2016, https://jonathanmckeewrites.com/age
-kid-phone.

16. Amanda Lenhart, "Teens, Technology, and Friendships," Pew Research
Center, August 6, 2015, https://www.pewresearch.org/internet/2015/08/06
/teens-technology-and-friendships.

17. "Screen Time and Children: How to Guide Your Child," Children's Health,
Mayo Clinic, February 10, 2022, https://www.mayoclinic.org/healthy
-lifestyle/childrens-health/in-depth/screen-time/art-20047952.

18. Bethany Thayer, "Family Meals: How Eating Together Boosts Health,"
Henry Ford Health, September 29, 2018, https://www.henryford.com/blog
/2018/09/family-meals-how-eating-together-boosts-health#.

19. Allison Engel, "Studying for Finals? Let Classical Music Help," USC News,
April 28, 2023, https://news.usc.edu/71969/studying-for-finals-let-classical
-music-help.

20. "Pros and Cons of Watching TV in Bed," *Forbes*, February 3, 2015,
https://www.forbes.com/sites/rent/2015/02/03/pros-and-cons-of-watching
-tv-in-bed/?sh=1517d02076da.

21. Julia Brailovskaia et al., "Finding the 'Sweet Spot' of Smartphone Use:
Reduction or Abstinence to Increase Well-Being and Healthy Lifestyle?!
An Experimental Intervention Study," *Journal of Experimental Psychology:
Applied* 29, no. 1 (2023): 149–61, https://psycnet.apa.org/doiLanding
?doi=10.1037%2Fxap0000430, cited in Adam Holz, "Reducing Screen
Time: A Surprisingly Simple Strategy," PluggedIn.com, April 29, 2022,
https://www.pluggedin.com/blog/reducing-screen-time-a-surprisingly
-simple-strategy.

22. Auxier, "Age of Screens."

23. Pew survey conducted March 7–April 10, 2018, cited in Monica Anderson,
"How Parents Feel about—and Manage—Their Teens' Online Behavior
and Screen Time," Pew Research Center, March 22, 2019, https://www
.pewresearch.org/fact-tank/2019/03/22/how-parents-feel-about-and-manage
-their-teens-online-behavior-and-screen-time.

24. "Digital Awareness for Parents," StopBullying.gov, August 17, 2021,
https://www.stopbullying.gov/cyberbullying/digital-awareness-for-parents.

25. Auxier, "Age of Screens."

26. Holz, "Of Algorithms."

27. Anderson, "How Parents Feel."

28. Steve Jobs, quoted in Pradip Thakur, *A Complete Biography of Steve Jobs*
(New Delhi, India: Prabhat, 2021), 218.

NOTES

CHAPTER TEN | THE RESET

1. Tristan Harris and Tim Kendall, quoted in *The Social Dilemma*, directed by Jeff Orlowski-Yang (Boulder, CO: Exposure Labs, 2020); also see Michelle Fitzhugh, "11 Noteworthy Quotes from *The Social Dilemma*," Redeemed Life Counseling, accessed June 8, 2023, https://redeemedlifecounseling .com/11-noteworthy-quotes-from-the-social-dilemma.
2. Julia Brailovskaia et al., "Finding the 'Sweet Spot' of Smartphone Use: Reduction or Abstinence to Increase Well-Being and Healthy Lifestyle?! An Experimental Intervention Study," *Journal of Experimental Psychology: Applied* 29, no. 1 (2023): 149–61, https://psycnet.apa.org/doiLanding?doi=10.1037 %2Fxap0000430.
3. Julia Brailovskaia, quoted in John Anderer, "Cutting Smartphone Use by Just an Hour a Day Improves Well-Being for Months," StudyFinds, April 22, 2022, https://studyfinds.org/smartphone-use-well-being.
4. *What about Bob?*, directed by Frank Oz (Burbank, CA: Touchstone Pictures, 1991).
5. Alex Kerei, "2023 Cell Phone Usage Statistics: Mornings Are for Notifications," Reviews.org, May 9, 2023, cited in Amanda Ruggeri, "How Mobile Phones Have Changed Our Brains," BBC Future, April 3, 2023, https://www.bbc.com/future/article/20230403-how-cellphones-have-changed -our-brains.
6. Kerei, "2023 Cell Phone Usage."
7. Jonathan McKee, *Parenting Generation Screen: Guiding Your Kids to Be Wise in a Digital World* (Colorado Springs: Focus on the Family, 2021).

CHAPTER ELEVEN | COMING TOGETHER

1. "Samuel Morse Demonstrates the Telegraph with the Message, 'What Hath God Wrought?,'" This Day in History, History.com, May 21, 2020, https://www.history.com/this-day-in-history/what-hath-god-wrought.
2. *Inside Out*, directed by Pete Docter and Ronnie Del Carmen (Emeryville, CA: Pixar Animation Studios, 2015).
3. *Till*, directed by Chinonye Chukwu (London: Eon Productions, 2022), quoted in Elliot J. Gorn, *Let the People See: The Story of Emmett Till* (New York: Oxford University Press, 2018), 59.
4. *Up*, directed by Pete Docter and Bob Peterson (Emeryville, CA: Pixar Animation Studios, 2009).

Keep being screen savvy.

You finished the book! You're ready to get on top of the entertainment and technology in your home. Just one problem...

New things come out all the time!

New shows. New games. Even new social media platforms. **There's no way you can keep up.**

...Or is there?

Don't fret. We here at Focus on the Family keep on top of that stuff so you don't have to. And you can access it all with *Plugged In*.

Focus on the Family's
Plugged In® reviews
help families like yours
navigate the world's
never-ending screens – and
all the unrelenting content we
see on them.

Get Christ-centered reviews. Learn
to manage technology and social
media usage. And make sure you're in
charge of the screens in your family's
life – not the other way around.

Scan here to explore